Malts & Jazz

Hans Offringa

Malts & Jazz

Conceptual Continuity

© 2013
Hans Offringa
Conceptual Continuity

Photography: Institute of Jazz Studies,
               Hans Offringa, Ben Williams
Design & Layout: Becky Lovett Offringa
Cover Design: Studio Baat

ISBN 978-90-78668-24-4

www.hansoffringa.com
www.thewhiskycouple.com

To Michael, Theo and Jack

- a formidable trio -

Table of Contents

FOREWORD

A Jackson in Your House

Whisky and jazz. It seems so obvious, yet somehow no one has written a book about it before. I can imagine our buddy Michael Jackson sitting there, nodding with approval as Hans explains his inspired notion that the two could be combined ... then beaming that he has done it so effectively. Jazz, after all, was MJ's music.

"Of course, you're not a jazz man," Michael said to me once. "Actually," I began, somewhat nervously (this was early in our friendship), "I started writing about jazz before I began writing about whisky." He looked at me over the top of his glasses ... "Really?" he replied, before giving me the most pleasant of exams, consisting of anecdotes of his meetings with Dexter Gordon, Ben Webster and all the other legends with whom he'd had a drink.

We began swapping tales, titles, musicians, finding that we parted company, jazz-wise, in the 1960s when I went off with Trane, Ayler, Shepp, Coleman (Ornette rather than Hawkins) and the "free" players. We could never quite resolve that, thank goodness, because it demonstrates how jazz is all encompassing, uncategorisable, open to all ... like whisky in so many ways.

Both are there to be explored. The book is never closed. Just as you think you may have reached your comfort zone, a new bottle, a new artist, comes along, jolts you out of complacency, offers up a new possibility, a new avenue to explore.

Neither does it matter that there is discussion between you and your friends over which malt is the best, because it opens up another area of dialogue between like-minded people. Malt whisky is all about conversation, comparing, talking, agreeing, disagreeing, learning. Jazz, likewise, is a musical conversation at its most intimate and, almost paradoxically, most intense. Listen to the music suggested in this book, see how the lines weave between the artists, the manner in which their musical voices rise, develop and subside. Jazz is about improvising on themes, just as every single malt improvises on flavours; the way in which every single cask offers a new interpretation of a distillery character is the same as a jazz musician bringing his (or her) own interpretation to a standard. To appreciate both you need to be contemplative yet alive to the moment, relaxed yet attentive, open to possibilities. Jazz is not background music; it sets the mood, it opens the mind. A glass of malt does the same. So does this book.

You pick malts in the same way as you pick your jazz. Writing this I looked for inspiration. Ben Webster? Too silky. Some Chet Baker? (MJ must have met him, surely) Nah, I'll just cry. I scan the shelves, Coltrane playing "Nature Boy," that'll do it. It's about matching the most appropriate tune to the time, mood and company in the same way as you'd choose the right dram for the moment. You wouldn't drink a heavy peaty malt as an aperitif, would you?

Choose your flavours as carefully as your music. Get the balance. Most importantly, take your time. Jazz is about playing with time, taking a theme, stretching it out, teasing and worrying at it, examining the possibilities of every note and in doing so, revealing the soul underneath. Likewise, a great single malt needs time, first to develop in the wood, then to open in the glass, to breathe, to unveil its depths and complexities. Malt isn't the three-minute head-rush of punk rock; it's a half-hour meditation on flavours as they expand, meld, then slow; it's about constant, subtle changes so that when you take that last sip and listen to that last chord you wonder: How did I arrive here?

As Trane's put back on the shelf, I spot an old Art Ensemble of Chicago record close by. It's called, appropriately enough, "A Jackson in Your House." Have an Offringa in your house as well. Thanks Hans ... there's hope for the whisky book after all!

Dave Broom

INTRO

Jazz is not dead,
it just smells funny!

– Frank Zappa (1940-1993)
composer, conductor and guitarist

Whisky isn't dead either; it's alive and kicking as never before. New markets emerge where the drink of drinks was not obtainable until recently and hedonistic pleasures are combined with a dram, like smoking cigars with a glass of fine single malt.

Whisky and food has become another matter of interest to whisky aficionados around the world. And indeed, some people do think that whisky smells funny!

There are more similarities between whisky and jazz, however. Both were crafted under the suppression of a neighbouring majority that looked down upon the craft as well as the craftsmen. The illicit stills in the Highlands paradoxically flourished due to the English suppression and eventually produced the most appreciated, most powerful expression – the single malt. Jazz was born out of traditional folk music brought by African slaves to the Americas and first considered a raw and uneducated form of "noise" by the majority of the white population in the U.S., only decades later to be embraced by that same crowd.

With my late friend and fellow writer Michael Jackson, I shared not only the love for the drink but also a passion for jazz in general and the bebop variety in particular. During one of our many get-togethers, he told me a story about him and Dexter Gordon, back in the 1960s in Amsterdam, visiting jazz clubs and chasing Lagavulin, which happens to be one of my favourite single malts. That story triggered my imagination and I invited Michael to my favourite pub in Zwolle, De Tagrijn. He immediately took a liking to publican Theo Dragt, owner of an immense collection of jazz cds and a lover of the cratur too. That night, 14 November 2004, the seed was sown for *Malts & Jazz*. When working on the manuscript, a few years later, I was assisted by another dear friend, Jack McCray, jazz historian and musician from Charleston, SC. Without this unique trio this book would not have become what it is. Unfortunately I lost all three of them in this world. They successively passed away in 2007, 2008 and 2011, all three too young, all three at home, all three due to a heart attack.

Whisky and jazz have proven to be survivors, regardless which drink or what musical style is the fad of the day. And these two survivors continue to meet, day after day, year after year. Whisky still is a favourite drink among many jazz and blues musicians. Alas, I cannot consult my three dear friends anymore, but fortunately I can book-shelf their memory. Enjoy the read.

Hans Offringa

THE ORIGINS

The Roots of Jazz

African Americans invented jazz music – even though it wasn't called jazz at the time – in the late nineteenth century in the southern region of the United States. Famous cradles of jazz are New Orleans, Louisiana and Charleston, South Carolina. The latter, with its undiluted enslaved African population, complete with the related retentions and residuals of African culture, was to play an important role in the future development of jazz, solidly founded in the African cultural concept of improvisation. Its roots, however, go back much further in time and are based upon traditional African folk music, brought to America by people from the West Coast of Africa. Being sold as slaves upon their arrival, they held no possessions whatsoever and were unintentionally forced to use the only instrument their masters could not take from them: their voice.

This original folk music existed in two forms of expression: religious chants that accompanied rituals and secular songs sung during monotonous labour tasks. The religious chants eventually would, under the influence of Christianity and the Africans' evolution of their own worldview, slowly transform into spirituals and gospels, whereas the work songs found their way to jazz via the blues. The latter two still hold much in common, albeit that the blues today is more closely connected to the original African roots than contemporary jazz.

Jazz is not African. It is not European. It comprises

elements of both, in terms of notation, instrumentation, presentation as well as expression.

After the abolishment of slavery in the USA in the 1860s (it was not banned in Brazil until 1888) African Americans gradually obtained more freedom and hence were able to possess things, including musical instruments. It gave a boost to their music. Many African Americans played either the trumpet or other horns, usually in marching bands. When classically trained New Orleans Creoles started to associate with the former slaves at the turn of the century, they brought the clarinet and the piano and started to fill in the "blanks" for which the slow, march oriented songs left optimal room. Similar situations existed in other places that were cradles of jazz. For example, classically trained blacks in Charleston, South Carolina, interacted with amateurs who contributed their own flavour to the tune. Around 1890-1900 a mixture of musical influences had led to two different musical styles known as "ragtime" and "blues."

Trumpet player Buddy Bolden, born in 1877, is often credited for being the inventor of jazz as a musical style. Around 1906 he was at the top of his fame, playing in New Orleans' red-light district Storyville as "King Bolden" Unfortunately, he couldn't cope well with his success and was taken to an asylum shortly thereafter and never again played a single note outside those walls. Creole Jelly Roll Morton, born in 1890 and playing the Storyville circuit too, unrightfully claimed that he invented jazz. However, this ragtime-blues pianist, singer, minstrel and all round entertainer was the first to write jazz compositions on paper. His "Jelly Roll Blues" (1915) was the first jazz work in print. He travelled all over the USA to popularise his music, mostly in Chicago, and paved the way for many contemporary musicians.

Although music recording was introduced in 1901 by the Victorola, it was not until 1917 that the first jazz song in history was recorded, "Livery Stable Blues," played by the Original Dixieland Jazz Band.

James Reese Europe (what's in a name?) was the first black bandleader to surprise Europe with march music influenced by jazz in 1918. In France and Belgium his band played to boost the morale of the military. The band was the 369th Regimental Band attached to the French Army. Its bandmaster, Francis Eugene Mikell, and others from Charleston were members of this famous band. Civilians were equally amazed with their mixture of march and early jazz.

On the other side of the Atlantic, jazz was introduced in the living rooms of many Americans via radio and gramophone. The music slowly evolved from Dixieland into all kinds of varieties, not all of them considered straight jazz by puritans. By the 1920s "hot jazz" was the talk of the town in Chicago. Young white people took an interest and started to visit the Southside bars to listen to their black heroes. Around 1924 in Chicago white trumpet player Bix Beiderbecke joined The Wolverines jazz band with saxophonist Frankie Trumbauer.

Bandleader Paul Whiteman integrated classical music with jazz and commissioned a composition from George Gershwin. In 1924 his "Rhapsody in Blue" was performed for the first time. White folks embracing jazz showed that this musical style, with its original African roots was now fully accepted in the white man's world. At the time bandleader Nick Larocca even claimed the white man invented jazz in an attempt to falsify history.

New Orleans natives clarinettist Sidney Bechet and bandleader King Oliver would have proven otherwise anyway, since they had been around for a while. The former took playing the clarinet to an entirely new level. The latter had a fine young trumpet player in his ensemble who would make an indelible stamp on jazz music for the next 50 years. His name was Louis Armstrong and he is considered one of the two greatest jazz musicians so far. Armstrong was born around 1900 in a rough neighbourhood in New Orleans and at the age of 12 was placed in a "correctional orphanage" after having fired a gun in the air, just for fun. In the institution he learned to play cornet. These places were often breeding grounds for musical talent.

Probably the most famous one is Jenkins Orphanage, founded in 1891 on the Charleston peninsula by Reverend Daniel Joseph Jenkins. It had an excellent music instruction program to keep the "inmates" busy. By 1895, one of Jenkins' bands had already toured in Europe with great success. Many of the unsung heroes of jazz who ended up in ensembles like Duke Ellington's, Count Basie's and others, came from South Carolina and literally played influential parts in the development of modern American music. Today's older Charlestonians still have a vivid recollection of the Jenkins Band, whose members danced, sang and played instruments on downtown street corners. In traditional African culture there is no separation between song and dance. This phenomenon culminated in 1923 in the iconic American song-dance music classic "The Charleston", written by James P. Johnson. The orphanage remains active today but no longer has a musical program.

The other giant of jazz was Louis Armstrong's contemporary Edward Kennedy "Duke" Ellington (1901-1974), who came from an entirely different background. He was born in Washington, DC to an upper middle class family. His father worked as a waiter in the White House and afterwards started his own catering service. At the age of seven, Edward received his first piano lessons from his mother. From an early age he enjoyed dressing sharply and earned his nickname "Duke" at high school. Duke Ellington was extremely talented as a pianist, orchestra leader and arranger, and composed evergreens like "Mood Indigo" and "Satin Doll." Around 1925 he started to perform in New York City with his own Duke Ellington Band. The Duke, however, preferred to speak about his music as "American Music" instead of jazz.

In 1924 Armstrong, nicknamed "Satchmo" (an abbreviation of "Satchel Mouth," as his fellow musicians sometimes called him), left Oliver's Chicago band, moved to New York and started to play with Fletcher Henderson. It proved to be an important stepping stone in his career as a bandleader. Soon he played the stages of many American music halls with his own groups.

The 1930s marked the rise of the Swing Big Bands with famous bandleaders such as Benny Goodman, Chick Webb and Glen Miller. Around 1936 John Hammond, one of the greatest talent scouts jazz and blues ever had, heard on his car radio a new sound, broadcast from Kansas City, Missouri. A new kind of swing entered his ears, and he drove down to check out the tunes. In Kansas City he found Count Basie and his Barons of Rhythm playing swing music heavily marinated in the blues. He convinced the Count to come with him to New York and bring his band with him. Among these musicians were the legendary tenor sax player Lester Young and a phenomenal guitarist named Freddie Green, one of Charleston's many unsung heroes, playing in the shadow of the big and famous. He would stay with Count Basie for almost 50 years. In the late 1930s the legendary singer Billie Holliday would join Basie's band for a year and once said that Freddie Green was the only man she really loved.

Meanwhile, Duke Ellington and Louis Armstrong crossed the Atlantic and conquered Europe, inspiring many young musicians to take up jazz. Guitarist Django Reinhardt would create his own style, called Hot Club de France. The nearing outbreak of World War II forced the American musicians to return to their homeland. Thus they could witness the saxophone becoming the most important solo instrument in jazz. The man responsible for that fact was Coleman Hawkins, who had toured Europe in the mid-1930s and played with Django Reinhardt for a while. With his 1939 recording "Body and Soul," he revolutionized the role of the saxophone in jazz, and in doing so became one of the front men of the bebop era, playing next to South Carolinian Dizzy Gillespie and North Carolinian Max Roach on the first bebop recordings ever.

Musicians like Charlie Parker and Kenny Clarke joined Gillespie, spearheading the bebop revolution, which lent room for long solos and interpretations of singular players rather than strict compositions played by a full-blown orchestra. Evolving alongside bebop, cool jazz, also known as west coast jazz, developed around Los Angeles and San Francisco, most notably by people like Chet Baker, Stan Getz, Dave Brubeck and Paul Desmond. It was slower, quieter, with fewer high notes and missing the hard-driving bop beat.

Around 1945 the Swing Era, which had been ruling jazz for more than 20 years, slowly lost its hold. Singers such as Frank Sinatra and Sarah Vaughan came to play an important role. The big orchestras disappeared from the stage. Smaller ensembles took their place. In the late-1940s alto saxophonist Louis Jordan would take the first steps toward rhythm and blues with his Jump Blues style, performing highly danceable tunes like "Caledonia."

Another variation on the new theme was called hard bop, exemplified by Art Blakey & The Jazz Messengers. Gillespie went along. So did Miles Davis, further developing bop into modal jazz and recording the landmark album *Kind of Blue*.

John Coltrane would later be influenced by the free jazz movement, developed alongside the hard bop in the 1950s and 1960s, led by musicians such as Ornette Coleman, Eric Dolphy and Archie Shepp. Free jazz, the adjective being somewhat out of place for a music already based on individual freedom of expression, would eventually lead to avant-garde, by many critics not considered jazz anymore. The 1960s also gave birth to Latin jazz and soul jazz. The former was heavily influenced by Afro-Cuban as well as Brazilian jazz, which is based upon the samba, rooted in the black songs from the last half of the Caribbean 1800s. The latter jazz style, often referred to as Bossa Nova, was shaped by rhythm & blues and gospel, played by trios or quartets. It often featured an organ or a guitar. Famous Latin jazz musicians are for instance Titu Puente and Joao Gilberto, with whom tenor saxophonist Stan Getz dallied and also recorded with Joao's wife Astrud. "Bashin" Jimmy Smith (Hammond organ) and Stanley Turrentine (tenor sax) are reckoned to belong to the group of soul jazz musicians.

Meanwhile, Louis Armstrong kept on playing, sharing the stage with the new generation, until he died in 1971. He didn't live to see the next innovation on the theme. Duke Ellington would continue to do his own thing entirely, composing right up to his death in 1974. By then the Duke was finally and rightfully acclaimed as the most important composer of American music.

When jazz met rock in the early 1970s, a style known as Fusion developed with famous front men like guitarist John McLaughlin, electric bass player Jaco Pastorius, violinist Jean Luc Ponty and keyboards player Herbie Hancock. Miles Davis, the continuous innovator, went along with them and created milestone records like *In a Silent Way* and *Bitches Brew*. McLaughlin would later even incorporate Indian influences in jazz.

Pop groups, including Chicago and Blood, Sweat & Tears, embraced jazz. From the latter band came Randy Brecker, who would form the famous Brecker Brothers Band in 1974, with his brother Michael, an alto saxophonist sometimes compared with John Coltrane. Even avant-garde composer, conductor and guitarist Frank Zappa arranged a considerable amount of his compositions to be played in a jazzy setting, like on the albums "The Grand Wazoo" and "Make a Jazz Noise Here."

In the 1980s straightforward jazz went into a decline, regardless of the unstoppable Art Blakey's attempts to keep this style alive. It was the decade of "smooth operators" like Grover Washington, Sade and Kenny G. This smooth form of jazz would ultimately deform, via acid jazz and rap jazz (rappers sampling original recordings from Charlie Parker and the like, adding their own thing to it) into lounge music at the beginning of the 21st century, performed by musicians such as Kruder & Dorfmeister and St. Germain.

Today jazz – and its history – is taught at prominent music colleges all over the world. Great jazz musicians lead in teaching, including Wynton Marsalis, considered by many as one of the best trumpet players currently around.

Research findings from the Charleston Jazz Initiative indicate that the beginnings of jazz and other points on the continuum of Black music are in rich abundance along the Gullah coast, southern North Carolina to northern Florida with Charleston at the epicentre. All of jazz's antecedents were in place on plantations, praise houses during moments of play. What happened in and around Charleston with regard to Black music rises to, or perhaps, exceeds what went on at the top of the Caribbean Basin (New Orleans, Louisiana) or around the Mississippi Delta (Memphis, Tennessee). For instance, the first documentation of the body of work that's come to be known as Negro Spirituals came out of Beaufort and Hilton Head Island, small South Carolina towns down the Atlantic coast from Charleston.

Charleston's Society for the Preservation of Spirituals, founded in 1923 and still active today, recorded songs from the fields and praise houses, gave the recordings to the Library of Congress and documented the words and music, compiling them in a book called The Carolina Low-Country (MacMillan, 1931). Spirituals, chants, work songs, field hollers and popular American music such as rags all evolved into what is now known as jazz. While jazz is not exclusive to African Americans, it is from that culture that it arose.

Straightforward jazz still inspires musicians everywhere and pieces written in the late 1940s till the early 1960s remain on repertoires of many contemporary ensembles and quartets. I have a preference for straightforward jazz. So did Michael Jackson. Needless to say that fondness reflects in the choice of the musicians featured in this book.

The Etymology of Jazz

Although jazz nowadays is strictly associated with music, the word entered the 20th century American language as a slang word in sports. In April 1912 the pitcher of the Portland Beavers talked about a new curve ball he had developed that year. He called it the jazz ball in an interview with the LA Times, "because it wobbles and you simply can't do anything with it." Other journalists quickly picked up the word and broadened its use as an adjective describing a certain energy or enthusiasm, but didn't connect it to music immediately. That would happen around 1915.

As with many slang words, schools and universities were the first to adapt it in everyday language. Around 1917 it was fully in use as a word in the realm of music, for example in names like "The Original Dixieland Jazz Band." At the beginning the word was sometimes written as "jass," but that spelling went into oblivion. Some sources indicate that it meant "j(ack) ass," hence the transformation to "jazz," possibly demanded by record companies who didn't want to be accused of using disputable expressions. But from where does the actual word originate? There are several stories about the root of the word jazz. It's been mentioned as stemming from the French verb jaser, which translates into chatting or chattering. It's been referred to as a term in gambling with dice, but also as coming from t'as, an Irish term for tea, meaning heat.

Coming from Storyville, the red-light district of New Orleans, the term might be associated with Jezebel, a 19th-century term for whore. Along the same lines, some people referred to jazz's origins as coming from jasmine, the favourite perfume of the Storyville prostitutes. These theories are not supported by solid evidence however and may best be considered as urban legends.

The most likely explanation is that jazz derived from the 1840s slang word "jism," which meant "spirit" or "energy." Jasm would have been the bridge between jism and jass/jazz. The Historical Dictionary of American Slang supports this theory.

Whatever is true, one thing is sure. Jazz is lively, spirited and energetic, and probably always will be as long as there are musicians willing to play and share their interpretations with an audience.

Three Principal Characteristics of Jazz

"It don't mean a thing if it ain't got that swing." A famous line sung by many famous jazz voices. Swing is often referred to as a particular sort of jazz during a specific era (mainly the 1920s and 1930s). That's wrong, or at least incomplete. Swing is an important ingredient, if not the most important, of all jazz. It is a tension between rhythm and metre that doesn't exist in other forms of music.

There is also a lack of counterpoint in pure jazz, the cause coming from the roots of course. The African music that travelled with the slaves to America contained melody and rhythm, but the Africans did not use harmony. Different melodies were sung next to each other and different rhythms existed at the same time and were performed synchronously. Anyone who has attended a "djembe" workshop will remember how difficult it is to play his own rhythm part while listening to another part at the same time. African rhythms are built entirely differently than the ones in Western music. Syncopated rhythms are key to jazz.

Jazz is music, more often than not, played in the 4/4 time signature featuring quarter notes with a rhythmic emphasis placed on the second and fourth beats, thus creating syncopation. Over the years and into the modern era, the beats have been further and further subdivided by rhythmic innovators such as Louis Armstrong (eighth notes); Charlie Parker and Dizzy Gillespie (sixteenth notes) and John Coltrane (thirty-second and sixty-fourth notes) increasing the complexity of the syncopated rhythmic variations. Jazz is blues based, straddling the category of contradictions between lament and joy. It is sometimes Latin tinged. It can also be offered in ballad form.

A third definite characteristic of jazz is this: Not the written composition but the interpretation is the predominant factor of the music. Whereas Western classical music is played from written scores, conforming to a composer's intentions, jazz pieces are interpreted by soloists. The latter do not play from scores but follow a general pattern or theme. That same characteristic applies to the blues. Improvisation is key to jazz. It is a technique designed to make a song better, melodically and rhythmically, improving it – not "making it up as you go along," the most common meaning attributed to improvisation.

The Source of Whisky

The Irish claim they invented whisky distilling. To state it simply, whisky is distilled beer, which is made of barley, a food staple growing in abundance in Ireland for many centuries. So far the Irish claim makes sense.

In finding out more about the origins of whisky, it is inevitable to take a closer look at the history of distillation, which takes us back roughly 5,500 years. A couple of 20th-century archaeologists dug up a little clay pot in Mesopotamia. They examined it and concluded that it was a distilling device dated to around 3,500 BC.

How did the art of distillation come to the Emerald Island? A favourite story is St. Patrick (387- 461), brought distillation to Ireland in the wake of Christianity. His follower, St. Columba, supposedly took the art to Scotland a century later, when he set foot on Iona, from where he made many travels to the Scottish mainland. However, the first recordings of distillation in Ireland come from a much later date. They were written down in The Red Book of Ossory, assumed to have been compiled in the 13th or 14th century by an Irish bishop whose name is long forgotten. This leads to the assumption that the story of St. Patrick and St. Columba might not be true, or, at least highly speculative.

Around 1290 the French Bethunes, a famous family of physicians, moved to Ireland and changed their name to MacBeth or MacBheata (Beaton in England). The

MacBheatas were famous throughout Britain and possessed a vast library of medical books in Gaelic, translated from original Arabic and Greek manuscripts dating back to the 8th and 9th century. Since at the time distillation was primarily used for medical purposes, they must have had a thorough knowledge of the process.

Legend has it that the MacBheatas originally came to Scotland in 1300 via Ireland with Princess Agnes who married Angus Og MacDonald, Lord of the South Isles. This branch of the MacBheatas first settled in Kintyre but quickly moved to the Isle of Islay.

This story sustains the theory that distilling came to Ireland first, having been under way from Mesopotamia almost 4,800 years. It then quickly reached Scotland. The first written record on whisky in Scotland appears almost 200 years later in 1494 and has been quoted many times, "To Friar John Cor, by order of the King, to make aqua vitae VIII bols of malt." Cor was from Lindores Abbey in the eastern Lowlands of Scotland.

From the 1600s to the early 1800s, many Irish and Scottish farmers often used part of their barley harvest to make whisky. It was easier to transport, and they could make more money with it. Whisky also was used quite often to pay the rent to the landowners. Distilling had become a cottage industry.

The English are credited with inventing laws regarding distilling. To many Scots they were so harsh that distilling became an illicit activity. In 1824 a law was passed with which it became much easier and cheaper to obtain a license and gradually the Scottish distillers in the High-lands converted to legally practicing the art. What the Irish did is not clear. They claim to have the oldest working distillery with a license, given in 1608 to Bushmills, but the actual license was given to the county, not the distillery. The terrible famine in Ireland and the cruel land clearances in Scotland around the 1850s caused a steady stream of Irish and Scots to enter the USA and Canada. These immigrants brought their distilling knowledge with them. The Indians handed them an indigenous grain – corn, from which the immigrants started to make whiskey (the common American spelling). Today corn, or maize, is still the primary ingredient in almost all American whiskey, with the addition of rye, wheat and barley.

The European continent has a distilling tradition of its own. Generally speaking the more southern countries started to distil using fruits as the main ingredient. Grapes fermented into wine, which when distilled, produced brandy. The northern countries have been producing distillates based on grains for centuries. The Dutch are famous for their jenevers, the English for their gin, the Scandinavians for aquavit and the Russians for vodka. Germany, Austria and Belgium also have been producing schnapps from various fruits for a long, long time. For a couple of decades now, these mostly family-owned companies have been making whisky and whisky look-alikes as a side product. Currently there are more than a hundred micro distillers on the European continent who make whisky or pretend to. The Netherlands alone is home to a handful of whisky distilleries, of one is spawned by a beer brewer, another by a jenever producer and another one that started from scratch in an old barn, just like the old days in Ireland and Scotland.

The Etymology of Whisky

In the quotation about friar John Cor lies a plausible explanation for the root of whisky: aqua vitae, the Latin expression for water of life. In Scottish Gaelic it is referred to as uisge beatha (uisge = water; beatha = life). In Celtic Irish it is spelled uisce beatha or usquebaugh. Since the English couldn't pronounce Gaelic very well they anglicised it to uisky in the 1700s, later to become whisky. For several centuries the word was spelled "whisky" as well as "whiskey" throughout Scotland and Ireland. Whisky without the "e" clung to the Scots and was exported to Canada and Japan. Gradually the "e" went with the Irish who probably took their spelling to the USA.

Today only the Irish and Americans continue to spell "whiskey." Remarkably enough the US Bureau of Alcohol, Tobacco and Firearms defines "whisky" as the official spelling in the USA. Only a few, among which Maker's Mark, spell their product without an "e." The term bourbon became eponymous with American whiskey, but actually is a certain type of whiskey and does not encompass all varieties. It leaves out Tennessee and rye whiskey for example.

Scotch, which refers to whisky made and matured in

Scotland, suffers the same disorder. For the past 20-odd years, many different expressions of Scotch were launched and the terms describing them often lead to confusion. The Scotch Whisky Association redefined the terms in an attempt to make the terminology more transparent. Not everybody describes that change as an improvement. Currently the following Scottish whiskies are distinguished:

- *blended whisky*: a mixture of grain whiskies and various single malt whiskies;
- *vatted malt whisky*, also named pure malt or blended malt: a mixture of several single malt whiskies;
- *single grain whisky*: made at one grain distillery from maize (corn), rye, wheat, rye,
malted and/or unmalted barley;
- *single malt whisky*: whisky made from malted barley only at one specific malt distillery;
- *single cask whisky*: whisky coming from a single cask, obviously from a single distillery; the American equivalent is single barrel whiskey;
- *vintage whisky*: a limited edition, usually a single malt with a limited, one- time output; often the year of distillation and the year of bottling are stated on the label; in the USA it is often called small batch (bourbon).

Complicated? Whatever variety is in your glass, you can always call it whisk(e)y. No need to pronounce the "e"!

The Production of Malt Whisky

To make single malt whisky one only needs three ingredients: barley, water and yeast. Barley contains starch that can be transformed into sugars. Adding yeast to sugar creates alcohol. That doesn't sound too complicated. The process to make whisky out of that is much more complex and can be divided into the following seven steps: malting, drying, milling and mashing, fermentation, distillation, maturation and bottling. Whisky can be made from various grains in various places but single malt whisky is exclusively made from malted barley, at one specific distillery.

Of all the grains, malted barley renders the most flavours to the eventual whisky. Barley also contains a high level of starch. When the barley is malted, natural enzymes are formed, which help to convert the starch into fermentable sugars. Generally speaking we distinguish two types of barley: two-row, with one row of seeds on each side of the stalk; and six-row, with three rows of seeds on each side. The former type is mainly grown in Scotland and Ireland. The USA grows both types. On the Orkney Isles, northeast of the Scottish mainland, a third type is grown on a small scale: "bere," a short, sturdy and very old type of barley that can cope with the extreme weather conditions in this part of the world. Each type is subdivided into many different varieties.

Cultivating new barley varieties is a continuous process. Barley is prone to picking up fungi, even barley that was originally resistant. New forms are tested in the laboratory of the National Institute of Agricultural Botany (NAAB), whose headquarters is located in Cambridge, England. Testing takes at least two years before the new variety can be placed on the UK National List. It is also possible to have a new type of barley added to the EU Common Catalogue of Varieties. Therefore official tests are required in all EU Member States.

If a new variety performs well, the whisky industry might exchange it for its previous barley. Such a rapid change happened in the 1970s when Golden Promise was released. It conquered an 85% market share within two years. Nowadays the barley market is dominated by Optic and Chariot varieties but a few distilleries still insist on using Golden Promise, like Glengoyne. Their distillers are convinced that the type of barley does influence the taste of the eventual whisky.

However, the general assumption in the trade is that the type of barley is barely a factor of importance in regards to taste. Scottish whisky does not have to be made of Scottish barley. A considerable amount is imported from England and Australia. Usually the price is the deciding factor, although the malting plants do have to deliver the malt to their customers' exact specifications. Order descriptions are detailed to the point of expected yield of alcohol per ton barley taken in. Barley gives a creamy character and depth to whisky, often identifiable as the taste of sweet biscuits and malt.

Water is used at every phase in the whisky manufacturing process. Lots of water. It is one of the main reasons why so many distilleries are located close to a river or a spring. The contents of a glass of whisky, poured from a standard distillery bottling, consist of approximately 40% alcohol by volume (ABV), about 1% congeners and 59% water. Apart from the fact that water has to be pure and clean, its consistency seems to have hardly any influence on the eventual whisky that is made out of it. At least, that is the general opinion. But is that correct? The influence of water on the making of whisky has been fodder, or more likely fuel, for discussions among distillers and aficionados alike. A closer look at the journey that water undertakes from its source to the eventual glass shows which factors are influential underway.

This journey starts at the source and the condition of the surrounding earth. Water that streams through relatively light soil takes on many more minerals than water that makes its way over a rocky terrain. Each *terroir* contains different minerals. Some examples illustrate that nicely: the granite in part of the Speyside is very hard and contains hardly any minerals, resulting in very pure and soft water. In the Northern Highlands, for instance around the village of Tain, the extremely hard water is rich on minerals since it ascends through layers of limestone. On the Isle of Islay the water runs its course to the distillery over peat bogs that mainly consist of decayed seaweed and heather. Bushmills, in North Ireland has water coming from basalt and clay grounds. On the other side of the Atlantic, Kentucky bourbon is made from water that contains lots of calcium but not a trace of iron, the cause being the limestone soil that acts as a gigantic filter. Yamazaki in Japan uses water that is filtered through layers of gravel and clay. All these waters are truly different regarding composition and that must inevitably have consequences in the rest of the production process.

Malting

Water makes its first appearance in the whisky making process during the steeping of the barley, which is part of the malting, and helps converting the starch in the barley into sugars (mainly maltose). Before it can be used, the barley has to be malted. For two to three days the barley is steeped in large steel vessels containing water. The grain becomes soft and sticky and starts to germinate. Small sprouts grow from the kernels and the starch in the barley grain is converted into maltose (a kind of sugar). Once spread out on the malting floor, the barley is turned regularly to prevent over-heating. A handful of distilleries still turn the germinating malt manually by using a wooden spade (shiel) or a motorized device resembling a small lawn mower. Because of its labour-intensive character this traditional process is largely mechanised and centralized. Germination takes about a week during which time the "green malt" becomes saturated with natural sugars, out of which alcohol will be distilled later in the process. If different types of barley are used, for instance Chariot or Optic, they will be malted separately since the one variety absorbs more water than the other. Fluctuations in the water temperature influence the steeping process: the colder the water, the longer the barley takes to become saturated. The amount of calcium in the water will seriously influence the tempo during fermentation, later in the process.

Drying

Germination is stopped by means of drying the barley. That happens in a kiln, using hot air. When peat is applied as fuel for the fire in the kiln, the eventual whisky will carry a distinctive smoky flavour. Nowadays most distilleries buy their malted barley from large commercial maltings that produce their malt on precise specifications. A distiller can exactly specify the peat level resulting from drying and thus secure the consistency of his whisky's taste. One can purchase stocks of malted barley with varying peat levels. This gives the distiller the possibility of producing different expressions from the same stills, ranging from a non-peated to a heavily peated whisky.

A smoky note in whisky does not occur by using peated water but by burning the peat in the kiln during the malting stage. The desired peat level is specified in parts per million phenol (ppm). Ardbeg's malted barley for instance has a peat level of 55 ppm, whereas The Glenlivet only has 2 ppm. Glengoyne does not use it at all and is sometimes dubbed "The Unpeated One".

During this phase in the production process, the starch from the barley is converted into sugars. Malted barley is mainly sweet. During drying, a number of sulphur-containing elements may be absorbed by the malt. Peat containing sulphuric compounds imparts this flavour when used for drying the malt. In some whiskies this is desired, in others not at all. If such components are present, the whisky may smell of rubber boots, struck matches, spent firework or (rotten) eggs.

Milling and Mashing

In the next stage the malt is cleaned through a large sieve and transported to a mill that grinds it into a coarse kind of flour called grist. The grist is then mixed with hot water in a huge vessel, the mash tun. The maltose in the grist dissolves in the water and the remaining sweet liquid, called wort, is drained out of the mash tun. After cooling, the wort is ready for fermentation. The residue in the mash tun, "draff", is used for feeding cattle.

One could argue that distilling whisky is a "cradle to cradle" process. The draff goes back into the food chain. The cows eat it, than fertilise the land whereupon new barley is grown. Barley that will be sold to the distillers ...

Mashing needs a great deal of water, since it is a batch process that's repeated three or four times at various water temperatures. In this stage the quality and composition of the water is very important. For instance, if the water contains too many minerals, like copper or iron, problems may rise in the next phase during fermentation. The degree of acidity also has to be closely watched.

During mashing various compounds such as amino acids are released from the malt. They sometimes emit aromas like cloves or sulphur in the mash tun, but most importantly they are the forerunners of the esters produced during fermentation and distillation. Esters contribute to the aromas of flowers and fruit that can be discerned in almost all malt whiskies. When the mashing is finished, the sweet wort is drained off.

Fermentation
The wort is, simplified, a sort of sugar water that is now pumped to a wash back or fermentation vessel. The amount of calcium not only influences the pace of fermenting but also the creation of esters. Water that lacks calcium causes a quick and aggressive fermentation cycle, whereas calcium rich water does the opposite. Which esters come into being depends for a large part on the mineral condition of the (sugar)water.

Yeast is a single cell fungus that feeds on oxygen and multiplies at a dashing speed. This is called aerobic fermentation. Yeast is also capable of converting sugars into alcohol and carbon dioxide, which is called anaerobic fermentation. The anaerobic reaction between yeast and glucose is notated as follows:

$$C_6H_{12}O_6 \text{ (glucose)} \rightarrow 2C_2H_5OH \text{ (ethanol)} + 2CO_2$$

This is the core of the fermentation process when making whisky.

After the yeast has been added the liquid starts to foam and froth aggressively. As said, the sugars are now converted into carbon dioxide and alcohol. This starts a reaction with the acids from the malt, which creates esters and aldehydes. The aromas we associate with flowers and fruit come from a combination of many different esters. That's why n-pentyl-acetate has a distinctive aroma of bananas.

In the second half of the 19th century Emil Christian Hansen, a Danish physiologist, made an important discovery. During his work in the laboratory of the Carlsberg brewery in Copenhagen, he found out that yeasts were compounds of various types of fungi, from which specific cultures could be developed. This meant a breakthrough in biochemistry. Hansen's contemporary Louis Pasteur discovered the role yeast plays in baking bread.

The Latin name for yeast is *Saccharomyces cerevisiae* (Saccharo = sweet; myces = fungus). Currently there exist between 700 and 1,000 known species. Not all of them have the capacity to convert sugar into alcohol.

The yeast fungi appear on plants, in the open air, on the ground, in and on people and animals. Wild yeasts spontaneously multiply in nature, for instance rotting fruit, which can have an immediate impact on the feathered fauna. Birds flying into a window pane might not merely be disoriented but plain drunk after having eaten fermenting berries. In the production of whisky, wild yeasts are not favoured. Most Scottish distilleres use cultivated yeast from a commercial producer, ordered either freeze dried or in liquid form.

Three main types can be distinguished: distillers yeast, bakers yeast and brewers yeast. One produces more flavours, the other more alcohol. Originally the Scottish

distillers used a mix of the three. Creating the optimal balance was important. Nowadays most distillers exclusively buy distillers yeast, especially the Mauri and Quest varieties.

Yeast strains can be more than a century old. Where most Scottish distillers tend to neglect the importance of yeast, their American colleagues take great pride in the pedigree of theirs. They are convinced that yeast greatly influences the flavour of their whiskeys and keep their yeast strains alive on site, by feeding them a diet of ground up grains.

At one tasting we conducted in Charleston, SC, two friends attended who brewed beer in their spare time. They used a proprietary yeast strain, which they had given the pet name "Bruno". They kept him alive in their bathtub by giving him rye and malted barley at set intervals. An hour into our presentation, one of them suddenly left the room and returned home. His friend explained: "Bruno needs his supper."

Originally wash backs, or fermentation vessels, were made out of wood, mainly Oregon pine or Siberian larch. They have a long life span, around 60-70 years, after which they have to be replaced. Gradually most distilleries shifted towards stainless steel wash backs because of economic and hygiene reasons.

Distillers who switched from wood to stainless steel all claim it doesn't affect the eventual taste of the whisky. The "traditionalists" who stuck to wood, claim the opposite and emphasize on the microorganisms living in the wood, which would be destroyed when cleaning a steel vessel.

During fermentation various esters, aldehydes, acids and fusel oils come into being. They either evaporate, leaving the pot still and being integrated in the eventual whisky, or condense and are redistilled. A typical fermentation cycle in Scotland takes between 40 and 50 hours, but it can take up to 80 hours or more. This varies per distillery and this is one of the important reasons why The Glenlivet tastes different than The Macallan. Too short a cycle will not render enough esters and alcohol. Too long a cycle might propagate bacterial growth (mainly lactobacillus), resulting in a reduction of the alcohol percentage and a deteriorating effect on the taste. Lactobacilli mainly produce lactic acid and acetic acid.

During mashing and fermentation other, secondary particles or congeners appear. The amount is small but their effect on the taste, the character and the quality of the whisky is considerable. These congeners can be subdivided in four categories: acids, aldehydes, esters and higher alcohols, which play a different part in creating the character of the distillate. Too many aldehydes, for instance, deliver a nasty smell and ruin the taste. In general higher alcohols and acids add body to the whisky, whilst various esters don aromatic, flowery and fruity notes.

Typical aromas that appear during this phase are the scents of green apples and a whole array of flowers. The latter especially when the fermentation temperature is high. Sometimes a buttery note develops.

Prosaically described, fermentation is nothing other than changing the chemical structure of a liquid by using microorganisms. Fermentation is sometimes referred to as yeasting. The resulting liquid is called wash and resembles a heavy beer, containing approximately 7-9% alcohol by volume (ABV).

Distillation

The wash is pumped to a still house where the liquid will be distilled twice in large copper pot stills. After fermentation the liquid in the wash back contains 8-10% ABV, a series of chemical compounds, mainly esters and aldehydes, and a huge amount of water. During distillation the character of the whisky is defined. Again water plays a role that should not be underestimated. As soon as the pot stills are fired, water and alcohol engage in a subtle and complex interaction. During a distillation round the relation between water and alcohol changes continually. This has to do with the evaporation temperature of both liquids and the heat created inside the still. Alcohol evaporates at 188.6 ° F (87° Celsius) and ascends through the neck and lyne arm of the still, after which the alcohol fumes are condensed. When the stills are fired too forcefully it might happen that together with the alcohol fumes some solids disappear through the arm and mix with the condensed liquid. This can have far-reaching consequences for the eventual whisky. During distillation - due to the constantly changing forces between water and alcohol – changes in taste will occur from one batch to another.

Distillation normally takes place in two rounds. After the first round the liquid will contain approximately 20% ABV, after the second round Scotch contains 70% ABV and bourbon up to 79% ABV. In any case the distillate after two rounds still contains between 20 and 30% water.

The first round takes place in the wash still; alcohol, esters, aldehydes and acids are separated from the yeast, other impurities and the remaining water. As soon as the fermented liquid reaches a temperature of 87 degrees Celsius, the alcohols in the wash evaporate and ascend through the neck of the still. The alcohol fumes then condense in the form of a raw, oily liquid called low wines, containing approximately 17-21% alcohol. The low wines are pumped to the spirit still, also known as the low wines still, to be redistilled. This second still is typically smaller in size than the wash still.

During the second round of distillation the stillman has much more to attend to than in the first round. He has to catch the middle cut or heart of the run. For this purpose he uses a spirit safe that was introduced by the British Tax office in 1823 to prevent illegal tapping off. With the safe the stillman can assess the quality and density of the spirit and decide when he takes the cut. In some distilleries this process is computer controlled.

The first part of the distillate is called foreshots. They contain impurities and are collected separately to be redistilled in the next round. As soon as the liquid reaches the desired quality and alcohol percentage the stillman switches the tap to the spirit receiver. It takes a lot of skill and craftsmanship, since at this point during the process the quality of the eventual whisky is determined.

At the end of the second distillation the temperature inside the still increases. Several oily elements, the feints, evaporate. They may influence the flavour of the whisky in a negative way and are collected together with the fore-shots to be redistilled with the next batch of low wines from the wash still.

Seeing a copper pot still in a Scottish single malt distillery always is a fascinating sight. Each still differs in size and shape. The smallest industrial pot stills in Scotland can be found at Edradour. Their maximum annual output is 90,000 litres (23,775 gallons). The largest stills are located southeast of Edinburgh, at Glenkinchie. They can turn out a whopping 1.7 million litres (450,000 gallon) per annum.

Copper, by the way, is the first metal with which mankind got acquainted. In the beginning it was used in its pure form but later it was mixed with pewter, resulting in the alloy bronze. Its name is derived from the Latin aes cyprium, meaning "ore from Cyprus." This Greek/Turkish island used to be a famous place to dig for copper in ancient times.

Copper is what is called a transitional metal. In its pure form it is not overabundant in nature, but is found much more as a copper-containing mineral. Examples are covelite, malachite, bornite and chalcopyrite. Copper ore is currently won mainly in parts of South America and the USA. The chemical symbol is Cu and the atom number 29, for the fans of elementary chemistry. The first use of copper goes back more than 10,000 years, which was proven by excavations in current Iraq and South-Jordan, where archaeologists stumbled upon King Solomon's copper mines. That discovery was made in Kirbat-en-Nahas – Arabic for "ruins of copper."

Copper and bronze were used rather early in other parts of the world, for instance Egypt and China, in 3,000 BC and 1,200 BC respectively. Europe has been long acquainted with the metal as well. In 1991 a mummy was found in the Italian Alps. He was buried with a considerable number of weapons, among which a giant copper axe, which was later dated at 3,300 BC. The mummy – the oldest found example in Europe - was baptized Ötzi, after the Ötz Valley, where he was found.

In ancient times copper was primarily used for tools, weapons, jewellery and mirrors. Today it is applied for totally different things like coins, electricity wire, microwave ovens and musical instruments. Hey, some jazz echoing here?

Copper is also used in construction, as roof covering, pipes and valves. The Statue of Liberty is said to contain no less than 100,000 kilos of copper. When copper is exposed to oxygen, its colour turns into a very recognizable light green.

The whisky industry wouldn't exist without copper (neither would certain expressions of jazz). Various tools of the trade are made of it. When entering a the stillroom, you'll see copper everywhere. The pot still, a round copper kettle that is heated from the bottom, is said to have been designed by a Dutchman (!) around 1600. The basic design is still in use in modern day distilleries and hardly modified in 400 years. Copper is ideal for distilling since it is an excellent conductor and easy to work with for a smith. It is also a very good catalyst, interacting easily with the spirit, resulting in various chemical reactions, by which unwanted sulphuric components will disappear. A pot still basically consists of four copper parts:

1. the pot, in which the fermented wash is heated;
2. the swan neck, through which the alcohol fumes ascend;
3. the lyne arm or lye pipe, guiding the alcohol fumes to the condenser;
4. the condenser – an old-fashioned worm tub or a tube-and-shell, in which the fumes cool down and become an oily liquid.

The various sizes of all those parts of the distilling equipment all influence the eventual taste of the whisky in different manners. For instance the angle of the lyne arm plays its part. Small copper kettles with short necks interact more intensely with the spirit than larger ones with long necks. A small pot still usually produces a heavier spirit, whereas from a large pot still a lighter variety emerges. This has nothing to do with the quality of the eventual whisky but solely with the body.

Pot stills are heated in different manners: indirectly from coils with steam heating or directly fired under the still. The latter method can cause caramellisation on the bottom of the still. That also influences the taste and aroma. With the help of so-called rummagers – a kind of chain that is dragged over the bottom – the burnt residue is scraped off, including miniscule amounts of copper. In earlier days direct firing was the only method but indirect heating became more and more popular after its introduction around 1960. It's much more efficient (and safe) than an open fire under the still. Glenfarclas experimented with indirect heating for a while but returned to direct firing, since they were convinced the former method influenced the taste of Glenfarclas the wrong way. Modern-day direct firing works more like an electric stove – no more open fires.

Due to the endless stop-start cycle of heating-cooling-cleaning-heating and so forth the copper wears out. That doesn't happen evenly over the entire surface and that is why a pot still is seldom replaced in its entirety. It is more customary to change parts that are in need of replacement. With extra care for every detail the copper smith will make an exact copy of the part that will be renewed. A famous urban legend tells that even the dents in the pot still are copied.

The lifespan of a pot still is approximately 40 years. The still comes in three basic forms: lantern, pear and onion. All forms are used throughout the industry and usually the spirit still differs from the wash still in a distillery. Pairs of the same stills are nearly always similar in shape, with exceptions such as Laphroaig and Mortlach. The former has three small spirit stills and one large, which can contain twice the amount of the smaller one. Mortlach has a motley crew of stills, all different in shape and the distiller emphasizes that fact as it contributes to Mortlach's unique flavour. Mortlach is what we call a meaty dram.

Some distilleries use a "boil ball," a thickening between the belly and the neck of the still. It promotes reflux (the falling back of heavier components that are then redistilled). Another tool for the same purpose is called "purifier," as can be seen at Ardbeg. Lantern shaped stills and those with very long necks like Glenmorangie's, promote reflux. The result is a lighter spirit with respect to the body. Compare it with the muffler for a trumpet, which reduces the volume, if you will.

The spirit safe, in which the foreshots, the middle cut and the after shots (or feints) are separated, is also made of copper. Parts of the pipes and valves needed for transporting the liquid from and to the wash and spirit still are made of copper as well.

The column still is the antagonist of the pot still and often, but not always, made of stainless steel. However, the inside does contain copper in the form of perforated plates, through which the condensed liquid can drip back against the ascending fumes. Each copper plate can be considered a mini still, stopping the heavier fumes and letting escape the lighter ones to the next column still.

They work in pairs, at least in Scotland and Ireland, and are called "rectifier" and "purifier."

At the bottom hot steam enters the first column and ascends, meeting the fermented wash underway. The result is an exchange of components whereby the heavier ones fall back to the bottom and the volatile parts leave the column at the top. During the second round of distillation the fumes cool down when ascending through the copper perforated plates. At a certain level in the second column still the drinkable alcohol (ethanol) condenses and changes back into liquid form.

The Lomond still is a crossover between pot still and column still. This type of still was developed by Alistair Cunningham and Arthur Warren in Scotland around 1955. Cunningham worked as a chemical engineer for Hiram Walker, a Canadian distiller who owned quite a few Scottish distilleries at the time. Warren was employed as industrial designer. It was Cunningham's task to create a greater variety of whiskies. He invented a round still on which a water container was mounted. In the neck he installed three copper plates. Their position can be modified, vertically as well as horizontally, to promote or reduce reflux. The lyne arm is adjustable too, for the same purpose. However, the movable plates tended to stick, due to the deposit that occurred and the Lomond still didn't become popular. Currently there are only two surviving ones in the entire Scottish whisky industry – one at Scapa on the Orkney Islands and one at, yes, Loch Lomond Distillery, slightly north of Glasgow.

In the USA distilling works a little bit differently. Most American distilleries use a column still, known here as a beer still, for the first round of distillation, usually made of copper, but not in all cases. The second round is performed in a still that is appropriately named the doubler. This "kettle" resembles a pot still and is always made of copper. Another slightly different type is the thumper. It contains hot water, through which the alcohol fumes from the beer still are directed for purifying. When these fumes make contact with the hot water, a thumping sound can be heard.

There is one huge exception to the American rule and that's Woodford Reserve. It is the only American distillery that produces bourbon in traditional pot stills, triple distilled. The three stills were purpose-built at Forsyth's in Scotland. This coppersmith from Rothes, Speyside, started to design and build copper and stainless steel distilling vessels at the end of the 19th century. During its existence Forsyth's diversified and nowadays not only delivers stills and pipes to the whisky industry but also manufactures a whole array of products for the offshore and construction industry. With customers worldwide, Forsyth services them via three separate units – consultancy, design and production. Copper, however, was the basis of this sheer monopolist in the whisky industry.

Another important manufacturer of the copper distilling kettle is Vendôme Copper & Brass Works Inc., from Louisville, Kentucky. This company, founded more than a century ago, not only supplies the whiskey industry with distilling equipment but also fences, tanks and industrial pressure cookers to various other industries.

All in all, copper is indispensable in the whisky world, not only leaving visual traces on the retina. Looking at these huge working stills is an event in itself, time and again. But, minuscule copper particles also find their way to the glass from which we savour our whisky, making it a very tiny flavour component in the drink we enjoy so much.

I love the beautiful round copper shapes. During my extensive travels through Scotland, Ireland and the USA I was lucky to capture many of them with my camera, as you can see in the accompanying pictures. The Bank of Scotland even immortalized a pot still on their 10-pound note. It's the one at The Macallan. In doing so they not only used copper for their coins but for their paper money too! My love for the pot still reaches so far that I have a miniature replica on my writing desk, complete with worm tub, mounted on a piece of wood with a name plate reading: Dalwhinnie. That was the first distillery I saw in my life as a whisky writer. In other words, my acquaintance with the copper in the whisky industry took place at the Drumochter Pass, a remote and high place – the highest location for a whisky distillery in Scotland! And Dalwhinnie's pagoda's are made of ... copper!

My visit at Dalwhinnie distillery took a few hours. When I returned to the car, I put Thelonious Monk's *Straight, No Chaser* in the CD player, driving north as a happy man.

Cooling/condensing

When distilling it is custom to talk and write about "process water." During condensing the correct phrase is "cooling water." It usually comes from a different source than the process water, for instance from a nearby river. Sometimes seawater is used for cooling, but that didn't prove to be successful in one particular case. Laphroaig experimented with it but decided to convert to normal water when they found that the condensers deteriorated rapidly under the influence of the salt.

Cooling water doesn't affect the spirit directly, but indirectly. The industry uses two types of condensers. The first and most traditional method is the worm tub. A copper spiral or "worm" is immersed in a big wooden vessel containing cold water. The alcohol fumes are in the worm. The cooling water lets the fumes condense into an oily transparent liquid. The second method is called tube-and-shell and it works exactly opposite to the worm tub. Cooling water is flowing through the tube and the alcohol fumes move in the surrounding shell. Temperature fluctuations in the cooling water influence the consistency of the distillate. During the winter these variations are minimal, but in summer it can become so warm that the distiller has to take extra time to cool down the water before condensing. It may slow down the whole process.

During distillation and condensing many esters occur. Some are wanted, some not. It is the stillman who decides which ones, by determining the length of the middle cut. What happens in those hours the liquid is heated in the stills, is very complex and not fully understood yet. This applies to the next phase too, maturation, although that takes much, much longer. The colourless middle cut, selected by the stillman at 60-70% ABV is pumped to a filling station, from where it will be poured into oak casks.

Maturation

Hundreds of years ago the Scottish Highlanders seized every occasion to savour a dram: a funeral, a wedding or a birthday. A true Scot wouldn't ignore an opportunity presented. In that respect nothing much has changed over the years. The perception of whisky did change however. In former days it was common to drink straight from the still. It mustn't have tasted very nice in its pure form because herbs and honey were added to flavour the raw spirit. Then in the 19th century, stories emerge about the positive influence of maturation in wooden casks. In those days Elizabeth Grant of Rothiemurchus wrote in her Journal of a Highland Lady: "... whisky mild as milk ... long in the wood."

Slowly attention focused on the diversity of flavour and aromas. And the cask came with it. At the beginning of the 20th century a law was passed in Scotland, dictating that the distillate had to mature in casks for at least three years, to earn the name whisky. This particular law would not only heavily influence the industry, but the eventual product as well.

Before the end-distillate, called "spirit" or "new make" in Scotland and "white dog" in the USA, is poured into cask or barrel, a third type of water is used, referred to as reduction water. In Scotland the alcohol percentage will be diluted to 63.5% before putting spirit in casks. This standard makes it easy for the industry to swap casks without running into problems with the Customs Office. After all the tax is based upon the amount of alcohol in the whisky. If you exchange a 63.5% cask for a 70% cask, although in a bonded warehouse, you have to come up with the 6.5% difference in taxes somewhere along the line! In Kentucky the bandwidth for barrelled whiskey is 55-60%, but distilleries hardly swap casks at all.

The reduction water is demineralised and does not add any flavours. A higher alcohol percentage extracts more flavour compounds from the cask that typically dissolve in alcohol. Hence, more water takes more water solubles from the cask. During maturation approximately 2-3% of the contents of the cask evaporate yearly. It's called "the Angels' Share."

In Scotland it's mostly alcohol and in Kentucky, due to the extreme changes in temperature over the year, it's mostly water that evaporates. The result is that the ABV in casks maturing in Scotland diminishes per year and the percentage of alcohol in the Kentucky barrels increases. Guess which part of the world the Angels like most …

Most malt whiskies mature 10-12 years and often longer in purpose built warehouses. The type of cask, the size, the maturation time and the climatological circumstances all influence the flavour and aromas of the mature whisky. In Scotland distillers use mainly casks that

previously contained bourbon or sherry. Sometimes they use rum puncheons or port pipes. The casks are imported from the USA and Spain respectively. European oak used is called *Quercus robur*, the red oak and *Quercus petrea*, or sessile oak. In the USA the casks, or barrels as they are called overthere, are made of *Quercus alba*, the white oak.

A new life in Scotland
American law dictates that bourbon can only mature in new American oak barrels. This law was introduced decades ago to stimulate forestry and surrounding industries in the USA. The Scots profit from that regulation, since the surplus of used barrels has to go somewhere. A second-hand barrel costs approximately 65 dollars and is shipped to Scotland disassembled, in staves. Having arrived at its new habitat, the barrel is reassembled and often enlarged from 200 to 250 litres. From then on it is referred to as a cask or a "hogshead." Nowadays roughly 90% of all Scotch whisky matures in casks made of the American white oak.

After four to five years of service in the bourbon industry, the barrel-transformed-into-a-cask will be used three more times in Scotland, typically for a 10 to 12 year period. After that it is exhausted and the remaining wood is put to various uses. From acorn to retired cask takes a life span of 120 years. That's not too bad!

Another historical fact influenced the Scottish choice for ex-sherry casks. Until the mid 1970s the Spanish shipped their sherry to Britain in casks, to the ports of London, Bristol, Cardiff and Leith (near Edinburgh). There bottling, distribution and sales were done. The Scots, never afraid of a bargain, took care of the empty casks, acting as an early proponent of recycling industrial waste.

The various casks used are known under several names, due to their different sizes: quarter cask, barrel, hogshead, puncheon, butt. During the long, long years of maturation the whisky develops over 50% of its eventual taste. Remember, from malting through distilling is only a matter of weeks!

When the whisky matures for too short a period, the taste might be a bit raw and sharp. Too long can result in the wood dominating and the whisky will taste astringent, which can be compared with a red wine containing too many tannins. Some whiskies can endure a long time in the cask, 25, 30 or even 40 years. However an old whisky need not necessarily be tasty. It might collapse over time. It is the master blender's art that is important in this stage. The Scots use their casks 50 to 60 years and regularly rejuvenate them. A so-called first fill cask is used for the first time after it has contained bourbon or sherry. Logically it renders more colour, aromas and flavours than a second or third fill cask. When a single malt has a very light colour it is safe to assume the whisky matured in a cask that has been re-used several times. A single malt is usually a vatting of various casks (first, second and third fill). This is done for consistency purposes.

"Rejuvenation" is part of the work done at the cooperages. At one time almost every distillery would have had its own cooperage. Nowadays only a handful still has coopers on site. Among them are Glenfiddich, Glenrothes, Strathmill and Springbank. Diageo, the largest player, owning 28 single malt distilleries in Scotland, mostly takes care of itself in a huge cooperage in the southern part of the country. For the rest, the majority of the coopering is outsourced to the Speyside cooperage, the only independent cooperage left in Scotland, although it is owned by a more than 100 year old French company.

Visiting the Speyside Cooperage is an awesome sight. The many barrels and casks waiting for repair, rejuvenation or re-assembling, are piled sky high. The coopers are paid by the cask. Seeing them at work is awe inspiring. Not only the speed with which they move the barrels but also their craftsmanship. An apprentice has to work for at least four years before he will be appointed a cooper. He will go through all departments and once he is skilled enough, he has to undergo various tests to show his ability. When the examiner is satisfied, the newly appointed cooper will be baptised in a time-honoured manner. He is lifted into an open cask of which the sides are painted with tar. Then he is enthusiastically rolled around the cooperage by his colleagues. Tarred and proud he emerges from the "vehicle" to join the ranks of the professionals.

Most cooperages are closed to the public. The Speyside Cooperage is an exception to that rule. It is open to visitors from Monday till Friday throughout the year, unless it coincides with a festive day. It is like stepping back into the 19th century when visiting the place. Although various parts of the process are mechanised, much of the work is still done manually. It is a proud and ancient profession and well paid, I've been told on more than one occasion.

Old and tired casks are given a new lease of life by cleaning and re-charring them. As a consequence the wood is more receptive to interaction with the maturing whisky. Casks that are beyond rejuvenation are turned into garden furniture, which is sold in the shop at the cooperage.

China at one time imported old casks and turned them into wooden flooring. Simply for that reason I'd love to travel to China, enter a house and put my nose down, trying to discern the unmistakable scent of a genuine The Macallan impregnated wooden floor.

Pioneer builds speakers out of old whisky casks and markets them as Pure Malt Speakers. This is the ultimate product to listen to jazz and sip on a fine single malt at the same time.

The geographical location and the climatological circumstances surrounding the warehouse that stocks whisky are factors that come into play to regarding the taste of the eventual product. Dalwhinnie matures on a high elevation. The annual cold period is more extreme and longer than in the Spey valley. Highland Park matures on Orkney, with a relatively consistent climate and minor temperature changes.

During the years of maturation the wood breathes and the liquid inside expands when it is warmer, while it contracts at colder temperatures. The bigger the temperature changes over the year, the more intense is the interaction between liquid and wood. Most distilleries do not mature the majority of their whisky on site anymore. Instead they use central warehouses, located in the belt between Edinburgh and Glasgow. Only the part intended for bottling as a single malt might slumbers on the premises of the distillery. A nice indicator for knowing whether there is maturing whisky is the presence of a visible black fungus on the trees and distillery buildings. It feeds on the Angels Share.

Generally speaking, whisky matured in ex-sherry casks develops a fruity taste, whereas whisky from ex-bourbon casks tends more to honey, flowers and vanilla. The esters causing these aromas were for a considerable part formed during fermentation and distilling. The wood will enforce them over time, but also adds flavour components like nutty aromas (coconut, walnut, hazelnut) and spicy notes (cloves, cinnamon, nutmeg).

Bottling
During the maturation period the master distiller or master blender regularly draws samples from various casks to test the development of the whisky. At a given moment in time he decides that the whisky can be bottled.

Before the whisky of a certain year will be bottled, the master blender marries a certain number of casks together in a giant mixing vessel. This is to guarantee consistency in the taste of the whisky. The "honeymoon" lasts from two hours up until two months, depending on the master blender's preference. After that period the whisky is ready to be filtered.

The Source of Whisky

Most whiskies are chill-filtered, the process of lowering the temperature of the matured whisky and forcing it through a series of filters. This not only prevents irregular particles from ending up in the bottle, but it also removes some elements that might turn the whisky cloudy when water is added. The consequence is that certain flavour components disappear as well.

Before bottling, single malt whisky is usually diluted with demineralised water to 40-43% ABV. This does not affect the taste. Many distilleries also offer nonchill-filtered versions of their whiskies, bottled at cask strength. These expressions are referred to as "cask strength un(chill)filtered". The ABV might differ from 50 to 70%. It is recommended to add some water to such whiskies.

Not every whisky has the same colour. One is darker than the other. To avoid confusing the customer, many distilleries add caramel for colour consistency. The amount is so tiny that it cannot be noticed in the taste or the aroma. A familiar blended Scotch therefore always has the same colour.

As long as a bottle is unopened the taste of the contents will not change noticeably. The whisky can be held for an undetermined amount of time, as long as the bottle is well sealed. Once open, the contents will stay fine for two to three years. The whisky will not go bad, but the liquid will oxidise over time, resulting in the whisky losing flavour. The higher the alcohol percentage, the slower this process takes place.

Pouring whisky

To optimally enjoy a fine whisky, a special nosing and tasting glass is recommended. They come in various shapes and sizes, somewhat resembling a sherry copita. Because the top narrows, the aromas remain longer in the glass. Were the whisky served in a tumbler, immediately many nuances in taste and aroma would disappear.

Adding a dash of water changes the molecular structure of the liquid in the glass. The whisky will open and reveal more aromas. Too much water could drown the whisky. An exact measure is difficult to give. What is negligible to one can be too much for someone else and vice versa. A handy tool is the plastic pipette, with which one can add one drop of water at a time. Some nosing glasses come with a lid, to cover the contents in-between sips.

There is no law against adding ice to single malt whisky. It is a pity though, since ice will anaesthetise the palate and cools the whisky in a manner that most flavours cannot be easily discerned. On the other hand, ice may release some flavours.

A glass of single malt easily can rest for a while. After half an hour the whisky will smell different than at the start. That is perfectly normal, due to oxidation. Very old whiskies in the 40-50 years range might not benefit from such exposure. They tend to collapse when longer in the glass.

Three Principal Characteristics of Whisky

First of all whisky is a container word. It encompasses all kinds of whisky and whiskey. It doesn't say anything about the type of whisky. Neither does Scotch, apart from referring to a product that is distilled, matured and bottled in Scotland. As with jazz there are different expressions. Jazz has to have swing; whisky has to be made out of grains. Those may be maize (or corn), rye, wheat, barley (malted and unmalted) or a mixture thereof. The type of grain or the recipe defines the sort of whisky. In this book the only whiskies extensively presented next to a jazz musician are single malts, made out of malted barley only. However, there is still enough room for variation and improvisation.

During the second round of distillation, the distiller has to judge three different streams of spirit: the foreshots, the middle cut and feints. They do not run from the stills simultaneously but follow each other. Only the middle cut or heart of the run is what the distiller is interested in. The first part contains poisonous alcohols and the last part fusel oils. Both are not desired in the eventual whisky. The distiller, however, can vary the length of each run. In this way he influences the taste of the eventual whisky. Therefore each spirit made at every distillery has a unique flavour and aroma before it is left to mature in oak casks for at least three years to earn the name whisky. Compare it with a jazz solo – you can keep it short or stretch it.

A third characteristic is the individual cask. It is up to the master blender to pick casks for blending and bottling. Here the individual craft is more important than a written recipe. By years of experience and a natural feel and nosing ability, the blender chooses those casks whose contents are ready for consumption. The production pattern is generic, but the individual expression of each cask's contents is different. Blended they can make a fine single malt. Left alone and bottled as a single cask malt they will express the ultimate individual character of a whisky. A true improvisation on the theme. And jazz is the ultimate improvisational music.

THE BLENDS

Jazz was born
in a whiskey barrel...

-Artie Shaw (1910-2004)
American jazz clarinettist, composer,
bandleader and author

Alcoholic beverages in general and whisk(e)y in particular have always been part of the food staple for many an artist, politician and even royal. Some among them personalised their style with a specific brand. Keith Richards is famous for presumably carrying a bottle of Jack Daniel's wherever he goes. Bill Murray became forever connected with Suntory Japanese whisky when he played the main role in the road movie *Lost in Translation*. This famous Japanese drinks company also owns three Scottish distilleries, Bowmore, Auchentoshan and Glen Garioch.

Actor W.C. Fields once asked his companions, upon his return from the men's room to the table in his favourite restaurant, spotting an empty bottle, "Who drank my lunch?" Winston Churchill preferred Johnnie Walker Black Label. Being a heavy imbiber at times, he was reportedly addressed on his drinking behaviour during a party. Bessie Braddock, the British Labour politician, supposedly remarked that Sir Winston was drunk, to which he parried, "And you, madam, are ugly. But in the morning, I shall be sober."

Prince Charles chose Laphroaig as his favourite single malt and granted the distillery a Royal Warrant upon his visit in 1994. The whisky-loving Prince even sells his own blend called Barrogil, whose name is derived from Castle Mey in Caithness, his late grandmother's favourite hangout. Part of the proceeds is earmarked for The Highland Initiative to stimulate the sales of local produce.

The writers' guild has its way with whisky too. Welsh poet Dylan Thomas was only 39 at the time of his death in New York in November 1953. Throughout his short life, Dylan would boast about his drinking behaviour and once wrote, "An alcoholic is someone you don't like, who drinks as much as you do." His last words were reportedly: "I've had eighteen straight whiskies, I think that is a record."

Nobel and Pulitzer Prize winner William Faulkner once wrote, "Civilization begins with distillation." Another one of his famous quotes: "There are no bad whiskies. One is just better than the other." Faulkner's fellow authors Ernest Hemingway and John Steinbeck also took a liking to the "King o' Drinks" as Robert Louis Stevenson once paraphrased whisky.

However the man who blended jazz, whisky and words all together perfectly in one sentence was Arthur Jacob Arshawsky. According to his official web site, he "is regarded by many as the finest and most innovative of all jazz clarinettists, a leader of several of the greatest musical aggregations ever assembled, and one of the most adventurous and accomplished figures in American music."

This remarkable musician also wrote several books on music, as well as a novel *The Trouble with Cinderella* and a series of short stories, bundled in two separate issues called *I Love You, I Hate you, Drop Dead!* and *The Best of Intentions and Other Stories.* This prolific and multi-talented character would become famous as Artie Shaw.

There's something very specific about whisky and jazz. The one has swing and the other has grain at its base. Lack thereof does not deliver the true product.

Different rhythms occur and different streams run.

How to assemble them is the true art. A bad solo can ruin the piece whereas a bad cask can do the same with the whisky inside. The same applies to the opposite: A good solo and a good dram create true pleasure to the ear and the palate. However, they do not exist solely by themselves. Solos have to be welded into the song, blended with the other instruments on the stage. A single malt only can make a reputation for itself by being compared to others, preferably through a tasting enjoyed in good company.

Both whisky and jazz are acquired tastes, both products created by professional and dedicated craftsmen. On a micro-level it's about a single malt whisky blended with an individual musicians' performance. A deeper dive into the life and times of those great individuals might deliver even more comparisons and show a true blend of music(ian) and whisky.

On the following pages, I concocted some combinations myself. Blends composed of individual musicians and individual expressions of single malts. It's not about over-indulgence; it's not about prescribing the ultimate combination or being precocious. It's about enjoying the fine things in life. A beautiful dram of single malt heightens the joy of listening, whether it is classical music, rock, reggae, blues or jazz. And in reverse, drinking a special malt allows its taste and aroma to echo into the accompanying music.

Taste is as personal as it gets. The chosen combinations are my preferences. For the occasion I have given each blend a name that does right to the malt and the musician at the same time and added a blue note to go with my blends of choice. To honour and commemorate my dear friend, the late beer and whisky writer Michael Jackson (†), the tasting notes are blends of his and mine.

It wasn't an easy task to single out ten terrific jazz musicians and ten equally fine single malts. Choosing them automatically meant leaving out other favourites.

After careful deliberation and inspiring discussions with a couple of jazz friends who know their Be from their Bop, I made the following line up. Here they are, in alphabetical order:

Cannonball Adderley
Chet Baker
John Coltrane
Miles Davis
Stan Getz
Dexter Gordon
Milt Jackson
Hank Mobley
Charlie Parker
Art Tatum

The Blends

Then I imagined what whiskies I would choose to savour whilst listening to their music and ended up with the following list, again in alphabetical order:

Aberfeldy
Balblair
Bowmore
Bruichladdich
Bunnahabhain
Glenrothes
Jura
Lagavulin
Oban
Springbank

This exercise resulted in the ten musical recipes represented in this book. They might not necessarily reflect your taste, but whatever your musical and whisky preference, I can only recommend trying to blend whisky and music yourself, preferably in moderation. It's rewarding and highly enjoyable.

Brown Velvet
Milt Jackson with Balblair

Milton Jackson was one of the Founding Fathers of the famous Modern Jazz Quartet, that would tour uninterrupted for almost 25 years between 1950 and 1974. The other three members were Percy Heath (bass), John Lewis (piano) and Kenny Clarke (drummer), whom Conny Kay would replace in 1955.

Jackson's musical career is much longer and spans six decades. He was born on January 1, 1923, in Detroit, Michigan, and at seven started to sing gospel with his younger brother. At eleven Milt got piano lessons and played drums but had to stop soon since there was no money to sustain his musical education. At school he received more training and switched to playing vibraphone. Later, when he had already become a famous musician he would reflect upon that change by telling, "I ended up playing vibes because it is the instrument most like the human voice, with one exception: once a singer adopts a style, it doesn't usually change much, but with the vibes there is so much variation and you can endlessly improvise."

His professional career started in 1946, when Dizzy Gillespie discovered Milt and invited him to join his big band. That's where he met his later Quartet-companions. In 1974 the Modern Jazz Quartet was disbanded, but would eventually re-join in 1981 and exist till 1997. In between Jackson would tour with various little groups, playing with other jazz greats among whom Thelonious Monk, Coleman Hawkins, Charlie Parker and John Coltrane.

He was also a great lover of the slow blues, which reflected in his playing as well as the setting of his vibraphone's oscillator to 3.3 revolutions per second. In comparison, his colleague Lionel Hampton favoured ten revolutions. One of his most successful compositions, *Bags Groove*, turned into a jazz classic. His nickname "Bags" supposedly refers to the bag he carried on his back, containing his collapsing vibraphone, and his habit of staying up all night long. Soul and blues musicians knew how to find him, and he starred alongside Ray Charles and B.B. King on several occasions.

Milt Jackson lived in Teaneck, New Jersey, a suburb of New York. On the 9th of October 1999, the man who had never taken on drugs or heavy drinking, in contrast to so many of his contemporaries, died of liver cancer in St. Luke's-Roosevelt Hospital in Manhattan. *The New York Times* wrote in his obituary, "... Milt Jackson, the jazz vibraphonist was a member of the Modern Jazz Quartet for 40 years and one of the premier improvisers in jazz with a special brilliance at playing the blues ..."

***

There are a wee number of Scottish distilleries that can trace back their history to the 1700s. Balblair is one of them. In the vicinity of a 4,000-year-old stone called *Clach Biorach* – Gaelic for sharp stone – local John Ross founded a small distillery in 1790 on the Balnagowan Estate. He soon turned it into a successful small-scale operation and welcomed his son Andrew into the company in 1824.

Apparently Andrew at first couldn't make up his mind where to go, since he left for nearby Brora distillery after a while, but returned in 1836 to take over Balblair because of his father's demise. Andrew continued to run the business successfully. In 1872 it was time for a thorough renovation. New buildings arose and the original ones were confined to housing casks of maturing whisky. Unfortunately Andrew died a year later. His son James took over the business but decided in 1894 to work for another distillery. Since James's sons weren't interested in whisky distilling, the license from Balnagowan Estate was taken over by Alexander Cowan. The new owner decided to move the distillery closer to the railway and built an entire new one, not too far from the old buildings. It was designed by the famous architect Charles Doig, the inventor of the pagoda chimney roof, that distinctive landmark on distilleries throughout Scotland.

However, in 1911 things went downhill rapidly and Cowan couldn't pay the wages anymore. Balblair ceased production. Until 1932 the former employees managed to sell the entire stock after which there was no sign of life on the distillery grounds anymore.

When eventually the entire Balnagowan Estate went bankrupt in 1941, the distillery was offered for sale. It would take seven years before a new owner showed up in the person of Robert Cumming, a lawyer from Keith. In 1949 the spirit flowed from the stills again, after a 30 year silent period. The new owner built up Balblair in the next two decades and was ready to sell the business in 1970. This time the tiny old distillery would become the property of Hiram Walker, who decided to add a third still.

Through a merger with Allied Vintners in 1988, Balblair was officially owned by Allied Distillers, eventually becoming Allied Domecq in 1994. The beautiful tiny old distillery seemed to become a pawn on the chessboard of the international drinks companies. Two years later plans were made to mothball Balblair for the second time since its existence, but the British-Spanish drinks company eventually found a new owner in Inver House Distillers in 1996. Five years later Balblair would become a Thai company when Inver House was taken over in 2001 by Pacific Spirits (UK), currently called International Beverage Holdings Limited (InterBev). It is the international branch of the Thai Beverage Public Company Limited (ThaiBev), via Inver House also owning the single malt distilleries of Pulteney, Knockdhu, Speyburn and Balmenach.

Throughout its existence, Balblair has put out various expressions of single malts, among which Elements, a 10 year old, a 12, a 33, a 38 and a 40-year-old, the last two being extremely limited editions. The company decided to replace all existing distillery bottlings and introduced three vintage versions, Balblair 1979, 1989 and 1997, soon to be followed by newer expressions. Independent bottler Gordon & MacPhail carries a 32 and a 40 year old version.

Although Balblair has known a troubled history, the distilling archives were well kept from the start and are one of the oldest in the industry. The first entry in the distillery ledger is dated 25 January 1800. It is from founder John Ross' own hand and reads, "Sale to David Kirkcaldy of Ardmore, one gallon of whisky at £ 1.8.0d." Those were the days, those were the prices ...

***

Blue Note
Milt Jackson had endurance, forming the Modern Jazz Quartet in 1945 and performing with his colleagues until 1997, albeit it with a break of seven years between 1974 and 1981. His playing was clean and straightforward. He was one of few musicians of his generation who did not indulge in drugs. Instead he let his music speak, spicy bebop complemented by the velvety touch on his vibraphone that became his trademark.

Balblair has stamina, too. It's one of the oldest working distilleries in Scotland. The whisky it produces is spicy, yet wonderfully soft. The clean environment in the Northern Highlands gives this dram a very agreeable lift.

Recommended listening
"Mean to Me"

Recommended dram
Balblair 16-year-old

Tasting Note
Pale amber. Nutty aroma, light, fresh spiciness. Fragrant. Firm, smooth and textured, surprisingly satisfying. Saltiness and shortbread (chocolate). A light whisky but packed with flavours. The finish is reminiscent of toffee and apple with a cedary dryness.

Eternal Innovator
Miles Davis with Bruichladdich

Miles Davis's official web site has a section that opens with a beautiful statement about one of the most important trumpet players in modern jazz history: "Miles Davis was the "Picasso of Jazz," reinventing himself and his sound endlessly in his musical quest. He was an artist that defied (and despised) categorization, yet he was the forerunner and innovator of many distinct and important musical movements."

Born in Alton, Illinois, on May 26, 1926, in a well-to-do family, Miles Dewy Davis III moved with his parents to St. Louis, Missouri, in the following year. His father was a dentist, his mother Cleota an amateur blues pianist. Apart from a dental practice, his father owned a large farm, where young Miles would learn to ride horses.

Despite the fact that his mother didn't reveal her capacities as a pianist, Miles rapidly showed great musicality. At the age of 13, he started to follow lessons with a local trumpet player who happened to hate vibrato. Every time his young pupil would use this technique distinctively, the teacher would slap Miles' knuckles with a ruler. Elwood Buchanan, as he was called, can therefore be credited with pressing Miles to play the clear notes that would become his signature throughout his entire career as a professional musician, regardless of what style he'd play.

Miles already played trumpet professionally at the age of 16, while still attending high school. After having graduated Miles moved to New York in 1944, under the pretense of studying at the Juilliard School of Music. No sooner had he hit the Big Apple (the moniker actually invented by jazz musicians in the 1920s), than he sought out Charlie Parker who invited him to play in his bebop quartet.

Three years later Miles formed his own nine-piece band and started to experiment with "new" instruments to jazz at the time: the tuba and the French horn. Not feeling at home in the bebop realm, Miles took a step further, and around 1950 he began to develop a style that would signal The Birth of the Cool. In the early 1950s, he also picked up the habit common with his musical scene: a heroin habit. In 1954 he conquered his addiction by going "cold turkey" at the family farm in St. Louis.

Throughout his career Miles would change the composition of his bands frequently, from nonet to quintet or sextet. He used the stage to launch aspiring young musicians and was one of the first to advocate playing in a racially mixed ensemble. It didn't amuse everyone, which led him to state, "I'd give a guy with green skin and polka-dotted breath a job, as long as they can play sax as well as Lee Konitz."

Many musicians playing with Miles in the middle and late 1950s were or would become famous in their own right, like John Coltrane, Kenny Clarke, Milt Jackson, Charles Mingus, Wayne Shorter and Joe Zawinul.

In 1959 Miles recorded a truly historic album, featuring John Coltrane, Cannonball Adderley, Wynton Kelly, Paul Chambers and Jimmy Cob. Having become tired of the complex music and continuous chord changes in bebop, he set out to create a new style, called modal jazz, influenced by the ideas of pianist George Russell. *Kind of Blue* would become not only Miles Davis's but also jazz's bestselling record, having sold more then three million copies to date.

Kind of Blue was "constructed" rather than recorded from straight playing. The many takes were later edited and "copy/pasted" to the master tape. In later years Frank Zappa would use this technique extensively on his *You Can't Do That On Stage Anymore* concert series and dubbed it "xenochronicity."

When Miles started to work with pianist and arranger Gil Evans around 1960, his musical realm would expand to a mixture of classical music, jazz and film scores, of which *l'Ascenseur sur l'echafaud* is one of the best known. On *Sketches of Spain*, Miles's trumpet may be heard against an orchestra performing the classical piece *Concerto d'Aranjuez*, originally written for guitar and orchestra.

At the end of the 1960s, Davis would lead the evolution of jazz rock fusion and invited musicians like Chick Corea, Billy Cobham and John McLaughlin to the bandstand. The cooperation resulted among other recordings in the famous double album *Bitches Brew*. Unfortunately Miles picked up his heroin habit again so fiercely that he had to withdraw from the public eye for five years.

When he made his comeback after having overcome his addiction for the second time, Miles was fully immersed in electronic music. Influenced by the likes of Jimi Hendrix, he used wah-wah and other distortion techniques on his trumpet. He ventured into the pop realm in the 1980s covering songs from Cindy Lauper and Michael Jackson. His comment on doing this was: "Many of today's accepted jazz standards pop songs come from Broadway. I am only updating the 'standards' repertoire with new material." He continued to re-invent himself with *Tutu*, a record with samples and synthesizer, by some critics described as the modern counterpart of the classically oriented *Sketches of Spain*. Miles also kept composing film scores and even played a little role in two movies, *Scrooged* (1988) and *Dingo* (1991). The latter movie would be his swan song. Miles Davis died on September 28 that year, in Santa Monica, California. He is buried in New York at the Woodlawn Cemetery, The Bronx.

***

LOW WINES SPIRIT
2
CONTENTS
74
LITRES

SPIRIT
SAMPLE SAFE

With money from his late brother William III, Barnett Harvey set out to build a distillery for the legal heirs, his three nephews William IV, Robert and John. Most distilleries at the time were extensions of farm buildings, but not Bruichladdich, which was purpose built, as can be seen in its current layout. The Harveys already owned two more distilleries: Yoker in Renfrewshire, founded in 1770, closed in 1928, and Dundashill in Glasgow (1811-1903), so they knew their trade. They would own Bruichladdich Distillery until 1938. A takeover by a small consortium started a merry-go-round of owners coming and going until Murray McDavid acquired Bruichladdich in 2000, remaining the major shareholder of the company. In between five different owners had tried to make whisky here and the distillery was mothballed four times.

Murray McDavid meant business and appointed Jim McEwan, formerly at Bowmore, as production director. Jim is one of the true living legends in the Scottish whisky industry and an indefatigable ambassador for Islay and its whiskies. He is as colourful as the steady stream of different expressions that leave Bruichladdich. Two other shareholders, Mark Reynier and Simon Coughlin, have a professional background in the wine industry. It shows, since one of Bruichladdich's more surprising editions is the slightly pink Flirtation, a 20-year-old single malt matured in ex-bourbon barrels and finished in red wine casks.

Most releases are limited and fodder for collectors, although one has to have deep pockets to acquire them all. Bruichladdich WMD-II The Yellow Submarine is a very interesting edition. Although the name echoes a famous pop song, it has nothing to do with the "Fab Four." Bruichladdich's website tells the story. A local fisherman found a little yellow floating object about five miles from the distillery. It turned out to be a mini submarine filled to the brim with hi-tech spying equipment. The fisherman towed the sub to the nearby port, hoisted it from the water and notified the Ministry of Defence. The latter first denied being the owner, then denied it was lost, followed by a statement that it was impossible the fisherman could have found it on the reported spot and finally claimed it informed the Coast Guard about the loss. However, no one involved could remember. To date, the MOD has not made any attempt to reclaim the vessel.

An interesting story involves the USA's defense service and the Internet. Bruichladdich, known by whisky fans as "The Laddie", is proud to show its working environment and has installed several web cams throughout the distillery. Once the Defence Threat Reduction Agency (DTRA) was browsing the web for terrorist activities and, encountering the distillery web cams, thought they had discovered a chemical weapons plant. The reports of this story show that Bruichladdich knows how to create rumour around the brand.

In 2002 Octomore was distilled, the most heavily peated whisky in the world, with an astounding 80 ppm in the malted barley. For comparison, Ardbeg uses 55 ppm. Since 2003 the whisky has been bottled on-site, being the only distillery on Islay to do so.

My own experience with The Laddie and the internet was of a more peaceful nature than "monitoring production of weapons of mass destruction." In 2006 my oldest son Sietse worked with Jim McEwan for a month at the distillery, a 19-year-old boy's dream come true. A "concerned" father could actually see his son moving about, thanks to those same web cams that fooled the DTRA.

The Laddie keeps pouring out interesting editions at a dazzling speed! Innovation is the keyword.

***

Blue Note
Miles Davis will always be remembered as boldly pursuing musical styles, finding his own interpretation of jazz, not necessarily always appreciated by his audience. He emerged in the bebop era, instigated the Birth of the Cool, invented modal jazz and ventured into fusion and electronic pop music, eventually returning to straightforward jazz. He constantly reinvented himself, and his style of playing was ever lucid, regardless of the surrounding bands. His output of recordings is stunning.

Until 2012, when Bruichladdich was taken over by the French drinks company Rémy Cointreau, the distillery was led by men who are as inventive in making whisky and marketing their product as Miles Davis was in jazz. Mark Reynier and Jim McEwan were tireless in bringing the Laddie to the attention of a wider audience. The latter, being director of production, has poured out so many expressions that collectors and drinkers alike almost started to protest. The distillery not only caught the eye of the aficionado, but also of the British Ministry of Defence and the DTRA. Not everyone in the whisky world might like its approach, but true to its cause, Bruichladdich never forgets its primary concern: making whisky. Let's hope the French continue to honour that tradition.

Recommended listening
"So What?"

Recommended dram
Bruichladdich 15-year-old

Tasting Note
Bright yellow. Sea air, slightly sharp. Firm, cracker-like with a malty background. Starts with a clean and grassy sweetness, then manifests an astonishingly long, lively series of small explosions. Peppery. In the finish one detects underlying iron. Savoury. Appetizing.

Exclusive Dedication
Charlie Parker with Springbank

Live fast, die young. That would have been an appropriate epitaph for the man who'd earn his rightful place alongside Louis Armstrong and Duke Ellington as the most influential jazz musicians to date.

At first it didn't seem like that was going to happen at all. Born on August 29, 1920, in Kansas City, Kansas, Charlie didn't show a specific talent for music, and his parents did not encourage him to play an instrument. His father, an alcoholic, was hardly ever home; his mother worked full time at Western Union.

At the age of 11 Charlie picked up an alto sax and taught himself to play it. At 14 he joined the school band but not very successfully. He was laughed off the stage. A year later he left school and decided to become a professional musician. Playing in a jam session with Count Basie's band, he lost the key and was humiliated again. This time by legendary drummer Jo Jones, who threw his cymbal, aiming at the young saxophonist's feet.

As a reaction Charlie would practice for many hours a day, until he could play in all 12 keys, later to find out that in blues and jazz, usually only a few keys are used. By intense practicing he also developed an incredible speed, showing he could play Lester Young's solos at double speed. He earned his nickname "Yardbird," later abbreviated to "Bird," because of his fondness for chicken meat.

Committed to the cause, Parker joined pianist Jay Mc-Shann in 1937 and continued to play blues and jazz with his band for almost five years. He would play the New York and Chicago club-circuit frequently and was first recorded during this period. In 1939 Parker left the band and moved to New York, earning a living holding several jobs, working as a part-time musician and as a dish-washer, not surprisingly at Jimmie's Chicken Shack. There he met pianist Art Tatum who must have inspired him to play fast and pay attention to harmony, as can be heard in Parker's later style. In 1942 Charlie left Jay McShann and via a short stint with Earl Hines he teamed up with a group of young angry musicians. They were fed up with the swing sound of the big orchestras and wanted to play their own music. Bebop was born. "Bird" would make waves with the Dizzy Gillespie and Thelonious Monk, among others. The latter is credited with saying at the time, "We wanted a music they couldn't play." The "they" probably refers to the white swing bands of the late 1930s and early 1940s.

At first bebop wasn't appreciated much by various reigning jazz musicians of the older generation. They rejected the "intellectual approach" of this new sound and in return were nicknamed "mouldy figs" by the beboppers. The critical remarks didn't stop the ever determined Parker from pursuing the high life and his star rose.

Sadly this coincided with his becoming more and more addicted to heroin, a drug he started using as a teenager, after he had been treated with morphine in a hospital, recovering from a car accident. Often Parker would not show up, or too late, or even without an instrument, having sold it to score drugs. Legend has it that he once played a plastic Grafton saxophone during a session at the Savoy, since his fellow musicians couldn't find any other instrument on such short notice. Eventually his drugs abuse and excessive drinking led him to experience a nervous breakdown in 1946. Having run mostly naked, wearing only socks, into a hotel lobby after having set fire to his mattress in his hotel room, he was arrested and brought to the Camarillo State Mental Hospital.

Six months later he re-surfaced, playing and recording as never before, soon using drugs and alcohol in large quantities again. In 1949 Parker saw a dream come true when he was given the opportunity to record songs with a chamber orchestra. Having heard Stravinsky one time, he'd wanted to record with strings. The result was a unique Parker recording appropriately named *Bird with Strings*.

In the 1950s Charlie Parker had become a role model for many aspiring jazz and blues musicians. Not only for his musical capabilities but also for his destructive way of life. Many musicians would follow his path in later decades, burning bright but short: Janis Joplin, Jimi Hendrix, Jim Morrison, Keith Moon, Kurt Cobain and Amy Winehouse, to name a few.

When his two-year-old daughter died of pneumonia in 1954, Parker lost what little control he had regained over his habits. Eventually his unhealthy way of life caught up with him. He died in a New York apartment on March 12, 1955, only 34 years old, of pneumonia combined with a bleeding ulcer, undoubtedly caused by living in the fast lane. The coroner who later examined him in the morgue estimated his age at around 60 years. His zest for life killed him, but fortunately his many outstanding recordings made "Bird" immortal.

Contemporary musicians are still influenced by the man who is considered by many the greatest saxophonist of all times.

***

W S
No 1
CONTENTS
274 Ltrs

Estd. 1828

SPRINGBANK

L

Cam

S SPRINGBANK
DISTILLERY

⚠ **Caution**
Fork-lift
trucks
operating

All visitors
must report
to distillery
office

🚭

Campbeltown, on the tip of the Kintyre peninsula, has witnessed rocky times but showed to be a sturdy survivor through the ages. In the 17th and 18th century the name was almost eponymous with smuggling, the coastline with its many coves made an excellent hiding place for the men whose profession was once considered honourable. Whether it was illegal or not, that business meant an economic stimulus for this remote part of the Scottish mainland.

Times however changed after 1823 when a law was presented that made it much easier and cheaper to obtain a license for whisky distilling. Campbeltown flourished and legal distilling operations mushroomed during the following decades, culminating in more than 30 distilleries. By the mid 1800s Campbeltown was known as the "Whisky Capital of The World" and considered a whisky production region on its own. The small town bustled with life; it also served as a main port to Ireland and the Western Isles.

But times changed again and not for the better. By the turn of the 19th century, the whisky industry at large suffered a severe collapse, caused by the so-called Pattison crash in 1898. A large Edinburgh-based company led by the Pattison brothers not only tampered with the quality of the whisky but also with the accounting. The brothers went to trial and were sentenced to prison, but the whisky industry was punished too. For a time Scotch whisky had a bad reputation and Campbeltown in particular was hit hard. Combined with the coming of other means of traffic, most notably the railways, the port and all its immediate activities went into a steep decline. The post-war depression in the late 1920s and early 1930s did the rest. In 1934 the distilleries of Glen Scotia and Springbank were the only ones producing whisky. It would take 70 years before a third distillery joined their ranks.

Springbank's history dates back to 1828 when the Reid family founded the distillery, the 14th erected in Campbeltown. Within nine years the Reids ran into financial trouble, regardless of the whisky boom and were offered help by their in-laws, the Mitchell family. The latter bought the distillery in 1837, and since then, descendants of the Mitchells have inherited the business. In 1897 a William Mitchell had the audacity to open a new distillery called Glengyle. His brother John continued operation at Springbank. William was the less fortunate of the two. Glengyle closed in 1925, only having produced whisky for 28 years. From then on its buildings would be used for storage.

Springbank suffered and had to close between 1926 and 1933, but did start up production after that silent period. In 1960 the company closed its malting floors and began to buy malted barley from elsewhere. When the independent bottler Cadenhead came up for sale in 1969, they were added to the Mitchell portfolio. A few years later the distillery began to experiment with a heavily peated variety that ultimately would become known as Longrow.

The next decade (1979-1989) Springbank would be closed for the second time in its existence, albeit that the first Longrow bottling was launched during that period, in 1985. From 1987 the production started on a limited base, not to use full capacity until 1990. Two years after that Springbank decided to reopen its malting floors. In 1997 a third, un-peated, variety was added and named Hazelburn, after a very old Campbeltown distillery that had operated between 1796 and 1925 and was once owned by Sir Peter Mackie of Lagavulin.

In 2004 a little miracle happened. Glengyle arose from its ashes and was opened by Hedley Wright, Springbank's primary owner and a direct descendant of the Mitchells. The whisky made in that neat and tiny distillery, directly behind Springbank, cannot be called by its proper name, since another company owns the trade name. Therefore its whisky was named Kilkerran. That name can etymologically be traced back to the Kintyre peninsula, whose Gaelic name was Kinlochkilkerran, in English meaning "the head of the loch by the church of St. Kieran." Ah, the beautiful compactness of Gaelic ...

Springbank's standard bottling is a 10-year-old, flanked by a 100 Proof, a 15-year-old, two Longrows (10 and 14 years old) and a 10-year-old Hazelburn. Various limited editions have been launched, mainly wood finishes. Kilkerran's "oldest" distillate is whisky now, but not yet widely available as a single malt.

Despite the fact that it has only three working distilleries, Campbeltown survived as an independent whisky region. The distinctive tastes of Springbank and Longrow as well as the resurrection of Glengyle surely contribute to that state. As one of very few in Scotland, the distillery is still family-owned.

Blue Note
Charlie Parker is vintage jazz. The man who was as much a genius as an individual who entirely went his own way, left an unforgettable impression on everybody who heard him or played with him. You might not have liked him immediately or not at all, but you would never forget the acquaintance. Parker was a major innovator in American music, changing the face of American culture.

Springbank is vintage whisky. Family-owned since its inception, it takes care of all business itself, from malting to bottling. They produce whenever they want, regardless of the demand globally. Very limited and rare are the Jazz Edition, from an ex-sherry butt and the Blues Edition, a vatting of 6 ex-bourbon barrels, both selected by the author and exclusively bottled for The Netherlands. Springbank knows how to improvise and has a mind of its own too.

Recommended listening
"Ornithology"

Recommended dram
Springbank 100 proof

Tasting Note
Golden. Dried apricots, soon overpowered by buttery toffee and marzipan, finishing with a slight smokiness. Big and oily. Sweet oak, rich. Coates the palate. With water floral notes emerge, but leave the honeyed woodiness intact. Sweet lingering finish, complemented by a hint of smoke.

Exquisite Spiritualist
John Coltrane with Glenrothes

Undoubtedly John Coltrane was one of the most controversial jazz musicians and composers of his time. Born in Hamlet, North Carolina on September 23, 1926, he was raised in a large Christian family, which would be an enormous influence throughout his musical career. Coltrane was a multi instrumentalist. At a young age he started to play the alto horn. In high school he sang in the boys chorus and changed the horn for a clarinet. Listening to the radio and records played on jukeboxes he picked up his taste for jazz and switched to alto saxophone after having heard Charlie Parker.

At the age of seventeen he moved to Philadelphia to develop his playing. Two years later, in 1945, he was drafted for WWII and shipped to Hawaii, where he played in the Navy band, of which some rare recordings surfaced recently. At that time he must have been given his nickname "Trane."

He left the military in 1946 and started to play with various famous musicians, among whom his greatest influences, Charlie Parker and Miles Davis. From playing bebop he switched at the end of the decade to big band music, joining Dizzy Gillespie's band for a while. After having left the big band it didn't take long before Coltrane reappeared as a tenor saxophonist playing in smaller ensembles. As with many other musicians at the time, he took drugs and became addicted to heroin. In the years that followed, Coltrane played with various bands and musicians, like Eddie "Cleanhead" Vinson, and toured with Johnny Hodges.

When he joined Miles Davis around 1955, his fame as a saxophonist started to grow. He would later say, "Miles gave me great freedom." He developed a unique style of playing, blowing three notes at the same time, which the critics referred to as "sheets of sound." In 1957 Coltrane successfully dropped his heroin habit and became more and more interested in the spiritual side of life. The seed that was sown in his early youth began to bear fruit. Apart from playing the flute and the bass clarinet, Coltrane now also practiced violin and harp meticulously. In 1960 the first version of his Classic Quartet came into being and would see a change of different musicians over the years.

At the turn of 1964 the Quartet recorded his most famous piece, a four-part suite called *A Love Supreme*. It was his personal homage to God, the final part called *Psalm* and being a musical interpretation of an original poem to his Creator that Coltrane had written earlier in his life. His musical interests then shifted to free jazz and avant-garde music. He enjoyed playing with Eric Dolphy and Pharoah Sanders. His compositions turned into long spun pieces that often would take more than half an hour to complete. Solos could take up to 15 minutes. Not everybody loved his exercises in free jazz, sometimes drenched in LSD, and critics, among whom Coltrane's former musical companion Miles Davis, didn't think highly of it at all.

The spiritually moved saxophonist might not have

cared. He continued to stimulate young jazz musicians like Archie Shepp to explore the outer boundaries of avant-garde jazz. He solidly continued to believe in a universal approach of everything he did as a composer and performer.

In 1966 Coltrane would state in an interview that his music was "a whole expression of his being." Spiritually and musically he had developed himself into one of the most influential people on the jazz scene at the age of 40. Sadly, he died of liver cancer on July 17, 1967, in the Huntington Hospital on Long Island, N.Y. Posthumously he would receive various awards. In 1971 he was declared a saint by the Saint John Coltrane African Orthodox Church in San Francisco. In the 1990s and 2000s more awards would follow. But the greatest awards of all to him will probably be the continuous performances of his compositions, be it in movies, accompanying television series or on radio.

Taking stock of his impact, we recall this is the man who once said: "I would like to bring to people something like happiness. I would like to discover a method so that if I want it to rain, it will start right away to rain. If one of my friends is ill, I'd like to play a certain song, and he will be cured; when he'd be broke, I'd bring out a different song and immediately he'd receive all the money he needed." We can only wonder what he would have achieved had he been given a longer life.

***

Although William Grant & Sons bought Glenrothes in its foundation year, James Stuart actually initiated the birth of this high capacity distillery in the town of Rothes. Forced by a poor financial position, Stuart unfortunately had to step back. It was an ill start for what appeared an ill-fated distillery for a long time. Eighteen years after the feeble start the distillery caught fire and was severely damaged. The owners kept an optimistic view and doubled the still capacity when they repaired the buildings. Five years later in 1903, disaster struck again, this time in the form of an explosion. Again, extensive repairs had to be executed. Then it went quiet for a while, until 1922 when one of the warehouses caught fire. Fortunately, the fire didn't spread around the entire distillery, but again, repairmen had to be brought in.

Despite the series of accidents, Glenrothes drew the attention of the industry and became highly regarded for blending purposes, most notably for Cutty Sark. The period between 1963 and 1989 illustrates the growing demand for Glenrothes single malt. In three steps the still capacity was expanded from four to six, then eight and eventually ten stills. In 1999 The Edrington Group stepped in as a major partner and owns the distillery today. Well-respected London-based wine merchant Berry Brothers & Rudd owns a license to consign their own bottlings.

In 1994 BB&R consigned a beautiful series of vintages, starting with one from 1979; this is now a specialty of Glenrothes. The labels on the distinctively shaped bottle mention year of distillation and year of bottling. In 2007

the Select Reserve was presented, carrying no age statement at all. It is now the core expression of the distillery. Various independent bottlers have launched special
releases of different ages and wood finishes, for instance
a 21- year-old rum finish by Douglas Laing.

Glenrothes is a colourful, stylish whisky. Ronnie Cox,
global brand ambassador, contributes highly to this im-
age, always immaculately dressed, always a gentleman and
an excellent companion for a dram and an interesting conversation.

The appearance of a ghost is another interesting as-
pect of Glenrothes' history. One of the other distilleries
in Rothes is Glen Grant. A former owner, Colonel Grant,
fought in South Africa during the Boer War. He stumbled
upon a little orphan hiding in the bushes and decided to
take him to Scotland. "Byeway Makalunga" grew up in
Rothes and became the Colonel's errand boy. At the time
he must have been the sole African in this part of Scotland.
As a result he became widely known and even made it to
the village soccer team. He lived to a ripe old age and died
in 1972.

So far so good. However, seven years later a ghost began to appear on the Glenrothes distillery grounds after
a pair of stills was replaced by new ones. It was considered such a serious matter that a university professor was
flown in to study the phenomenon. He concluded that an
invisible energy line had been disturbed during the instal-
lation of the new equipment. He put it right and went to
the cemetery adjacent to the distillery grounds where he

ruminated in silence. He had never before been in this place but after a while he walked in a straight line to a single tombstone, approximately 70 yards from the distillery. For a couple of minutes he seemed to have a conversation with the dead. Then he returned and made it known that the situation had been resolved in a friendly manner. The name on the tombstone read "Byeway Makalunga."

His ghost did not reappear, but ever since the professor's creepy encounter, it has become a tradition at Glenrothes to daily make a "Toast to the Ghost." Talk about spirits...

***

Blue Note

John Coltrane expressed a deeply religious commitment throughout his life, fuelled by a thorough religious upbringing. When he'd overcome his drug addiction, he started to play more and more instruments, venturing into the realm of avant-garde jazz, culminating in beautiful recordings of an almost spiritual nature. Once asked what he wanted to do in the next decade, he answered, "I want to be a saint." Coltrane found himself through his art. He examined himself and his purpose in life and expressed his findings very elegantly. His tenor had big shoulders.

Glenrothes is an exquisite dram, in an extraordinary bottle. The highly respected and old London-based company, Berry Brothers & Rudd, owns a license to bottle Glenrothes for exclusive use. The dram itself is spiritual in more than one way. The distillery grounds were once visited by a real spirit who left after the intervention of a Scottish professor.

Recommended listening
"A Love Supreme"

Recommended dram
Glenrothes Select Reserve

Tasting Note
Pale gold. Oak, vanilla and coconut with a hint of prunes. Full, melodic. Rich malt, medium sweet, vanilla and orange peel. A light, but long finish.

Gateway
Stan Getz with Oban

The "mellow" man with the astounding, flawless technique and warm, poetical sound was born in Philadelphia, Pennsylvania on February 2, 1927. Soon afterwards the Gayetski family moved to New York. They had come from the Ukraine at the turn of the century and decided to Americanise their name to Getz. Stan excelled at school and started to play saxophone when he turned 13, albeit that he would enjoy playing on every instrument he got his hands on. Lester Young was one of his first musical influences. At 14 he was playing in his high school orchestra, which entitled him to get a free tutor from the New York Philharmonic Orchestra.

Turning 16 he became the protégé of Jack Teagarden and started to play with famous musicians like Nat "King" Cole and Lionel Hampton. Via gigs with Benny Goodman he became a soloist in Woody Herman's Second Herd. Their hit *Early Autumn* boosted his career and from 1950 on Getz would be the leading man in his own quintets and quartets. In 1953 he formed a sextet with Dizzy Gillespie. The two were joined by rhythm tandem Ray Brown-Max Roach as well as Herb Ellis and Oscar Peterson.

Starting as a teenager Stan Getz frequently used alcohol and drugs. He continued to do so until he got arrested in 1954 for an attempted robbery of a pharmacy, needing to score. In an attempt to become sober, he travelled to

Europe, where he stayed in Copenhagen for a while. When he came back to New York in the early 1960s, he teamed up with Charlie Byrd and got involved in Latin Jazz. During this period he made one of his most famous recordings, with Joao and Astrud Gilberto, *The Girl from Ipanema*. After his Latin affair he returned to cool jazz for a while. Then he joined bass player Stanley Clarke and keyboard phenomenon Chick Corea in the early 1970s. It meant a step toward jazzrock fusion, which eventually led Getz to experimenting with electronic gimmicks on his sax like audio delay and echo. The critics didn't like it and slowly Getz returned to acoustic jazz. In the last phase of his life, his music became more esoteric and he turned away from the Bossa Nova style of his 1960s success altogether.

Getz, nicknamed "The Sound," was often praised for his immaculate control of the saxophone, which he played with seemingly no effort at all. But in reality it meant working hard, as it is very hard to obtain such a level of perfection. John Coltrane once said about his colleague: "We would all play like that ... if we could."

Stan Getz was not only prolific in a musical way. In between travelling and playing concerts in Europe and the USA, he managed to father six children with three different ladies, two of whom he had married. His collaboration with the Gilberto couple ended after he had enjoyed a love affair with Astrud.

On June 6, 1991, the smooth operator of jazz and women died of liver cancer. In 1998 he was immortalized by a donation of the Herb Alpert Foundation, which made it possible to erect the "Stan Getz Media Center and Library" at the Berklee College of Music in Boston.

***

SPIRIT STILL
Contents
8296 Litres

DISTILLAT

WASH STILL
Contents
18880 Litres

A small urban distillery is nestled cosily in the centre of Oban, from which it takes its name. It seemed a rare location for a distillery since the overwhelming majority always liked the countryside better, for obvious reasons. Illicit stills were less easily detected in the hills and mountain ranges, when gaugers and excise men operated their detested practice: trying to find and demolish them.

Not so with Oban. On the contrary. The name, meaning "Little Bay of Caves" in English, had been an important port for many centuries to Picts, Celts and Vikings alike. John and Hugh Stevenson took a different approach. They were avid builders and entrepreneurs, raising an entire village around the distillery and the bay. The brothers soon owned various other businesses ranging from a slate quarry and factory to a fishing operation and a brewery, rapidly becoming the largest and virtually only employer in the area around the turn of the 18th century.

In 1821 Hugh's son Thomas inherited the conglomerate and hurried back from Argentina to claim his stakes. Not having the business instinct of his father, he ran into financial debts and had to file for bankruptcy in 1829. Luckily his son John took after grandfather Hugh and saved the distillery, managing to buy it from the creditors for the decent sum of £ 1,500 and running it successfully for more than 35 years. In 1866 local Peter Cumstie bought the distillery, probably as an investment, selling it 17 years later to James Walter Higgins, who started renovating and modernizing Oban in 1883. During the expansion, workers found human remains and tools in a cave behind the distillery. The findings would later be dated as stemming from the Mesolithic, about 6,500 years ago.

After the modernization the distillery slowly attracted the attention of larger players in the industry. In 1898 a conglomerate of various business people, among which the powerful Dewar-Buchanan clan, acquired Oban. The latter became part of the Distillers Company Ltd in 1925, which eventually would become an important cornerstone of Diageo.

Between 1931 and 1968 Oban struggled as a start-stop operation, mothballed a couple of times. After elaborate reconstructions the distillery reopened in 1971 and has not ceased to produce since. At first Oban was bottled as a 12-year-old single malt but that changed in 1988, when Oban became part of the original six Classic Malts. From then on the malt with the salty tang would be bottled as a 14-year-old. This expression is still the core version, only joined by a Distiller's Edition with an extra maturation in Amontillado fino ex-sherry casks. The distillery launched a couple of limited bottlings too, a 20 and 32-year-old version. Understandable, since Oban needs the bulk of its production for the highly appreciated 14-year-old. It is the second smallest of Diageo's nearly 30 distilleries, and there isn't really any room for expansion, since it is crammed between other buildings in town to the sides, the main street and harbour in the front and a sturdy rock at its back.

Although the distillery is a landmark in the village cen-tre, it is somewhat overshadowed by a remarkable building called McCaig's Tower, named after John Stuart McCaig, a local banker. He must have been something between an eccentric and a megalomaniac since he erected the building, which resembles a Roman arena, as a monument for his family. The story goes that when he died in 1902, nobody really wanted it. Instead it was nicknamed McCaig's Folly. A fact to sustain that theory is the building itself. Only the outer walls were erected. It makes Oban a very interesting little harbour town, easily spotted from afar. Oban is also referred to as the "Gateway to the Isles," serving an important role in transporting goods to and from Islay, Jura and Mull ever since the old Picts, Celts and Vikings roamed the countryside.

***

Blue Note

Stan Getz earned his nickname "The Sound" for his immaculate control of the saxophone, regardless of the style he played. He was a front man of the West Coast style, developed by Dave Brubeck. Soon Getz ventured in to the hard bop area, adding Bossa Nova to his list of accomplishments in the 1960s, travelling to Europe and experimenting with electronic jazz, but eventually returning to straightforward jazz. His music gently seduces you into listening, maybe in the same way he seduced the many women in his life. Getz was an amazing soloist, but he also performed well with others. This skill showed up in Woody Herman's Second Herd in 1947, which was very influential and helped propel him even more into the spotlight. Getz was one of the "Four Brothers" in the band, joining Zoot Sims, Serge Chaloff and Herbie Steward.

Oban developed itself not only as a distillery but also as a whole town, with supporting industries surrounding the grounds, even venturing into beer brewing. Its single malt is a soft seducer with a great balance. Due to its easy access to some of the Western Hebrides, Oban is also called the Gateway to the Isles. Stan Getz in turn can easily be called a Gateway to the Styles.

Recommended listening
"Blood Count"

Recommended dram
Oban 14-year-old

Tasting Note
Amber. A whiff of the sea, malty notes, a touch of peat. Firm but smooth, slightly oily. Starts delicate on the palate and perfumy with a hint of seaweed, developing into waxed fruit. Lightly smoky. The finish is aromatic, smooth, appetizing and slightly dry.

Gentle Giant
Dexter Gordon with Lagavulin

A giant among giants, almost 2 meters (6'5") tall. He was raised in a family where jazz celebrities the likes of Duke Ellington and Lionel Hampton would frequently visit to consult his father, Dr Frank Gordon.

Dexter Keith Gordon was born on February 27, 1923, in Los Angeles, California. He began to play the clarinet at age 13. Two years later he picked up the alto saxophone to exchange it for a tenor sax when 17. Soon after that, he received a request to join the band of Lionel Hampton. Apparently his father's old patient had not forgotten.

"Long tall Dexter" as he was called, left Los Angeles and started to tour with Hampton's band and travelled through the country, learning to play with the great musicians of the time. When playing in Chicago in 1941, he was first recorded. Two years later he played in New York City, still with Hampton's band, and was influenced by Ben Webster and Lester Young. According to Dexter this period was a turning point in his career and he soon became well known.

Shortly thereafter he moved back to Los Angeles and played with Fletcher Henderson. In 1944 he joined Louis Armstrong who would also greatly influence him. With sidekick Nat "King" Cole, he performed as the leader of a quintet. That same year he moved on and started to play with Dizzy Gillespie, Sonny Stitt and Sarah Vaughan in the

Billy Eckstine band. Now Dexter Gordon had become one of the great and early leaders of the hard bop.

As if this list was not impressive enough, he started to play tenor duels with Wardell Gray. These battles became a great commercial success. At the turn of the decade, Dexter turned up at the famous 52nd Street in New York, playing along with Charlie Parker and Max Roach.

In 1960 Blue Note Records asked him to start recording with them. In the five years that followed, he made numerous recordings with many musicians who would become famous later, including Freddie Hubbard, Bud Powell and Bobby Hutcherson.

After having played a session in Ronnie Scott's famous Jazz Club in London, he took a liking to Europe and would stay there for 15 years, living in Paris, Amsterdam and eventually settling in Copenhagen. It might also have had something to do with his earlier conviction for drugs possession and use, for which he had served time in his home country. In any case, Amsterdam took a more lenient approach to drugs. Moving to Europe didn't prevent Dexter from continuing to record with Blue Note, for which he frequently flew to the USA and back. Finally in 1976 he decided to leave Europe for good and return to his native country. He received an enthusiastic welcome in New York, immediately assembled a new band and started touring with them all over the country. According to Dexter, it was his best band ever.

In the mid 1980s his musical career led him into a different direction, when he played the main character in the movie *Round Midnight*, loosely based upon the life of Bud Powell. It would become an all time classic. Herbie Hancock won an Oscar for Best Music and Dexter himself was nominated for Best Leading Actor. The movie also meant reuniting with some companions of earlier times, since Bobby Hutcherson and Freddie Hubbard were two of the many musicians who played minor roles in the movie.

Until his death Dexter Gordon would always stay true to the style that made him famous, straight ahead bop, although during his stay in Denmark, he would unknowingly become connected with the heavy metal world, being the godfather of Lars Ulrich, many years later to be known as the drummer of Metallica.

Dexter Gordon died of kidney failure on April 25, 1990, in Philadelphia, Pennsylvania. It was Zoot Sims who delivered the perfect epitaph for the giant man, "Dexter always had that big sound, from the early days. He's a big man. Stands to reason, he's gotta lot of lungs."

***

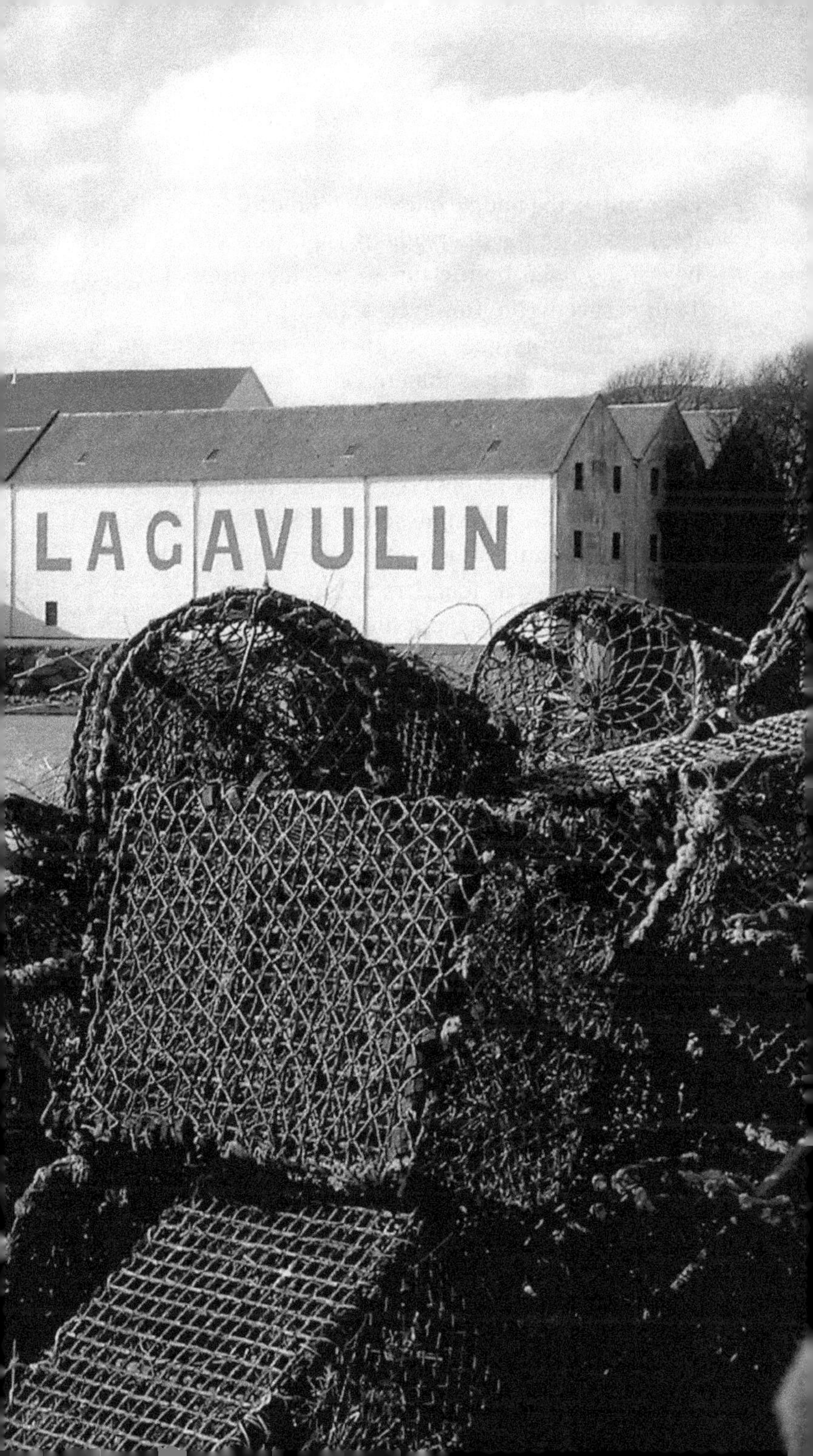
LAGAVULIN

Lagavulin is the middle one of the three Kildalton distilleries, flanked on the right side by Laphroaig and on the left by Ardbeg, who both claim to be older (from 1815 and 1810 respectively). However, according to local lore, the unofficial history goes back to 1742 when Lagavulin Bay was framed by no less than ten illegal rudimentary distilleries. At the time the whisky produced at this lovely spot was called "laggan mhoullin", which translates in English as "the mill in the hollow." The official founding took place in 1816 by John Johnston, sometimes wrongly mentioned in whisky literature as the father of Donald and Alexander, who are credited as founders of Laphroaig.

However, the history of both distilleries is highly intertwined. Around 1837 said Donald ran Lagavulin for a short while alongside his daily work at Laphroaig. When Walter Graham became Lagavulin's owner in 1852, he had been working as temporary manager for Laphroaig since 1847 when Donald Johnston had died, continuing to do so until Donald's heir, Dugald, came of age in 1856. Graham would quit working at Lagavulin in 1860 when the distillery was acquired by James Logan Mackie, who in his turn owned a license to trade Laphroaig. His nephew Peter Mackie joined Lagavulin in 1878 and introduced White Horse 12 years later. From 1890 till 1901 the famous blend with the white horse on the label was for export markets only. Then Mackie's blend also conquered Scotland.

Peter Mackie was deservedly nicknamed "Restless Peter." He was quite a character, matching boundless energy and grand vision with ditto ability to execute his plans and in the possession of a dangerously short fuse. In other words, a man who wouldn't give way to the devil himself. When Laphroaig ended his contract as an agent, Restless Peter went mad and sought revenge. That was partly understandable, since the Mackies had turned Laphroaig into a well-known brand worldwide during the previous 80 years. His first act was to block the water supply of Laphroaig. A court judge was needed to make him restore the waterway. It only fuelled his anger, and he lured Laphroaig's master distiller away. With the help of that unfaithful man, he built a new distillery within Lagavulin and named it Malt Mill. The stills were an exact copy of Laphroaig's. Mackie must have thought, "When I cannot sell it, I will produce it myself."

Apart from Lagavulin Mackie owned two other distilleries, Hazelburn in Campbeltown and Craigellachie in the eponymous Speyside village. During his life he never succeeded in damaging Laphroaig, and Malt Mill didn't even taste like it. Peter Mackie did receive a knighthood and could be buried as "Sir Peter" in 1924. A couple of years later, in 1927 Lagavulin became part of the Distillers Company Ltd (DCL) a forerunner of current owner Diageo.

The year 1952 was disastrous for Lagavulin when a raging fire destroyed a large part of the distillery buildings. Reconstruction fortunately didn't take too long. In the early 1960s Malt Mill was demolished and its site transformed into a visitor centre. Up until 1988 Lagavulin had been one of the lesser-known single malts, but the launch of the six Classic Malts brought this distinctive, yet elegant single malt under the eye of a broader audience. Lagavulin became so popular as a single malt in the 1990s that the standard 16-year-old was a scarce product for a while. Currently this expression is widely available again, due to a 24 hours, seven days a week production schedule. Lagavulin's core range consists of a 12-year-old cask strength version, the said 16, and the Distiller's Edition, basically a 16-year-old with an extra maturation in Pedro Ximenes ex-sherry casks. Several limited editions are available, among which a 21, a 25 and a 30-year-old. Nearly all output goes into single malt. Only a small percentage is reserved for blending, not surprisingly for Sir Peter Mackie's old stallion White Horse.

***

Blue Note

Dexter Gordon is credited by the late beer and whisky writer Michael Jackson (1942-2007) as the inventor of the Smoky Martini, which cocktail is made with Lagavulin. The tall, handsome and amiable tenor saxophonist has more to offer in this blend. His long, lingering, grand sound is simply made for the extremely long finish that makes Lagavulin loved by its fans.

Although very smoky, Lagavulin is not a hard hitter like its neighbours Laphroaig and Ardbeg. Instead that smokiness is held in a mild, almost velvety quality that makes this giant of a dram far more gentle than one would expect from a heavily peated Islay malt.

Recommended listening
"Round Midnight"

Recommended dram
Lagavulin 16-year-old

Tasting Note
Amber to dark orange. Sea spray, smoked fish, creosote, campfire on the beach. Full, with a velvety smoothness, very firm. Peaty dryness like gunpowder tea, developing into an oily, smoky, huge dram with hints of salty sea-weed. The finish recalls a warming peat fire. A bear hug. Almost never-ending.

Quiet Resourcefulness
Chet Baker with Bunnahabhain

Trumpet player and jazz singer Chesney Henry Baker, Jr. was born in Yale, Oklahoma on December 23, 1929. Around the age of 10 he started to play the trombone, a gift from his father, a professional guitarist. Chet would exchange the trombone for a trumpet after a while, the former instrument being too large for him to handle. In later years he would also adopt the flugelhorn.

The local Glendale Junior High School provided him with a bit of a musical education, until he left to join the Army in 1946, at the age of 16. Transported to then West Berlin shortly thereafter, he started playing in the band of the 298th Regiment. After two years he left and went to Los Angeles where he managed to study theory and harmony, but quit the El Camino College after a year to join the Army again. It didn't last long; the call to music was too great. He started to play in an Army band in San Francisco and was soon spotted in various jazz clubs, where he teamed up with Stan Getz.

It was Charlie Parker who boosted Chet's career as a trumpet player when he invited him to play in a series of concerts on the West Coast. Parker must have remembered him well, as some time later in New York he warned Miles Davis about "that little white cat on the West Coast."

Chet later joined the Gerry Mulligan Quartet, where he might have picked up his heroin habit. Within a year,

Mulligan was arrested for drugs possession and had to serve time. The Quartet had been a tremendous success from its start, and Baker continued to perform with his own groups for the years to come and would forever be considered a front man of the "cool jazz" of the West Coast.

In the 1960s Chet Baker moved to Europe where he soon was convicted for drugs use and possession, which lead to imprisonment in Italy and Germany. It was the start of a steep decline, and after several drug-related incidents, the trumpeter and singer was officially deported from Germany back to the USA. He returned to California and was convicted several times for petty crimes. The year 1966 marked the depth of his downfall when he was beaten up severely during a rip-deal. The remains of his teeth after years of heavy drug abuse were kicked out, and Chet lost his embouchure altogether. Slowly he learned to play with dentures, exchanging the trumpet for the flugelhorn most of the time, since it was easier to play. His playing style drifted into an early form of smooth jazz, combined with singing. His inimitable voice can best be heard on "My Funny Valentine."

After he regained his embouchure he returned to straight jazz and moved back to Europe in 1978 after a short stop in New York. The next decade he would only return to the USA for an occasional gig. In the early 1980s, Chet started to play with jazz musicians such as guitarist Philip Catherine and pop star Elvis Costello, with whom he scored a tiny hit in the UK and therefore was recognized by an entirely new audience.

Although his health suffered badly from his drugs abuse and he was sometimes unreliable about showing up, Chet Baker grew as a trumpet player and singer. In hindsight his last years proved to be his most mature ones, musically speaking. In 1987 he performed in Tokyo. The concert was recorded live and released after his unforeseen death in 1988. It's considered by many as one of his best recordings ever.

On May 13, 1988, Chet Baker died as result of falling from a hotel window, aka defenestration, in Amsterdam. There are several theories about his death, ranging from suicide to murder. For neither cause evidence was found. Autopsy results showed there were drugs in his body, and the police found a respectable amount of cocaine and heroin in his hotel room. A plausible explanation is him losing his balance when looking out of the window – most likely under the influence. One of the most lyrical trumpet players and jazz singers had literally left the building. A bronze plaque in the wall of the Prins Hendrik Hotel in Amsterdam marks the end of his life.

Chet Baker is buried at the Inglewood Park Cemetery in Inglewood, California.

***

N°1
WASHSTILL
CONTENT
35356

Nº 1
LOWWINES
STILL
CONTENT
15,546

The lightest of the Islay drams, with hardly a trace of the ubiquitous peat, is made at this distillery that once was surrounded by a whole village, even containing a school. Prior to its creation, the Mouth of the River, the English translation of the Gaelic Bunnahabhain, was a wild and uninhabited wasteland. The very building of the distillery brought about a lively little self-supporting community of distillery workers, their wives and children, hence the need for a school.

Although the warehouses look rather grim, Bunnahabhain is a lovely distillery where time stands still. The buildings are positioned in a beautiful location overlooking the Sound of Islay, that wild and windy sea street between Islay and the Isle of Jura, once used for bringing in supplies and taking away barrels of whisky. Nowadays that is done with tankers via the narrow and winding road that leads to Port Askaig.

In the latter part of the 19th century, the founders were already well connected in the whisky business. Robertson, from Robertson & Baxter, was a wine and liquor merchant, for a while even agent to Laphroaig on the southeast side of the island. The Greenlees brothers were two of the founding fathers of the Islay Distillers Company, which would merge with William Grant & Sons into Highland Distillers around 1887.

From 1930 till 1937 Bunnahabhain fell silent. After reopening, the two stills would arduously work in unison to make up for the lost years and were joined by a second pair in 1963. Approximately 20 years later Bunnahabhain was mothballed for the second time in its life, to be reopened in 1983-4 after two silent years. To celebrate the 100th anniversary, a 21-year-old was released, probably the first run from the four stills.

This doesn't mean Highland Distillers could not count, but instead of taking the foundation year as Bunnahabhain's first, they counted from the start of production, which was in 1883. Most distilleries tend to be a little vague about founding dates, which doesn't make life easier for a whisky writer.

In 1999 the Edrington Group took up the challenge and acquired Bunnahabhain, but almost immediately mothballed the distillery again. The spirit flowed through the stills only a couple of weeks per year for the next four years.

Bunnahabhain's water is piped from streams in the hills and does not flow through peat. The resulting whisky is very light and has virtually no peaty influence, due to the unpeated malted barley that has been used for so long. However, just before selling Bunnahabhain to Edrington, Highland Distillers did some experimenting with a peaty version, which would be introduced on the market in 2004 as a 6-year old named Moine, but not by Edrington. In 2003 they sold the distillery, together with the famous blend Black Bottle, to Burn Stewart Distilleries.

Throughout its life Bunnahabhain's output went mostly to the blenders. Only a small percentage matures on-site and will end up either in one of the single malt expressions or in Black Bottle, which contains all Islay malts.

Bunnahabhain's 12-year-old has readily been available over many years, supplemented by various limited editions and the much appreciated 18- and 25-year-old versions that are part of the core range now. Bunnahabhain launched commemorative limited bottlings on various occasions, most notably a 33-year-old Auld Acquaintance in 2002. Several independent bottlers among whom Signatory released Bunnahabhain at various ages. In 2010 a rare hand-numbered 30-year-old was released by the distillery. It comes in a beautiful leather case, accompanied by a pewter quaich and a certificate.

The distinctive label on distillery bottlings features a sailor behind the captain's wheel, with the caption "Westering Home," after a famous local song that starts like this:

Westering home and a song in the air
Lights in the eye and its goodbye to care
Laughter o'love and a welcoming there
Isle o' my heart my own one

***

Blue Note
Chet Baker was one of the most lyrical trumpet players ever. His beautiful melodic phrasing and tender voice merge well with this quiet single malt, the lightest of the Isle of Islay. Chet would stumble and fall, but recover in his late years, by many considered to be his best musically. It took time for him to mature fully.

Bunnahabhain has a chequered history, somewhat resembling a struggle to survive, comparable with Chet Baker's life. Fortunately, Bunnahabhain is still going strong and excels in vintage expressions. It is a whisky that matures well at a great age.

Recommended listening
"Let's Get Lost"

Recommended dram
Bunnahabhain 12-year-old

Tasting Note
Golden. Remarkably fresh, sweet sea-air aroma. Light to medium, but firm. Gentle, clean with a nutty-malty sweetness. Very full flavour development in the finish. Refreshing.

Showcase
Cannonball Adderley with Aberfeldy

Alto saxophonist Julian Edwin Adderley was born in Tampa, Florida on 15 September 1928. As a little boy he was nicknamed "cannibal," later to be transformed into "cannonball," perfectly suiting his rather portly posture as a grown man.

Julian's father was a trumpet player, and he must have inspired Julian, who studied music in Tallahassee from 1944 until 1948. After that period Julian started to work as a band director and music teacher at Dillard High School in Fort Lauderdale.

In 1955 he moved to New York with the intention of attending graduate school. The intention was good but died instantly when he sat in with the Oscar Pettiford Band in Manhattan's Café Bohemia. It propelled him into a musical career on the jazz stage. With his younger brother Nat, who played the cornet, Julian formed his first quintet. It wasn't a success commercially, but Miles Davis noticed his playing, and in 1957 he would become a member of the trumpet player's legendary sextet, playing alongside John Coltrane and Bill Evans, among others, for the next two years.

In 1959 Cannonball formed his second quintet, again with brother Nat, and became an overnight success at San Francisco's Jazz Workshop. His musical approach shifted to soul jazz, and in the one-and-a-half decades to come, the quintet was regularly enlarged to a sextet, featuring musicians who would rise as giants of jazz on their own accord, like keyboard players Joe Zawinul, later to become a member of the famous jazz rock group Weather Report, and George Duke, who joined Frank Zappa's Mothers of Invention in the early 1970s for a couple of years.

Cannonball would continue to play funky jazz for years to come and scored a great hit with *Mercy, Mercy, Mercy*, composed by Zawinul. To broaden his approach, he also started to play the soprano sax. Late in life he returned to straight jazz, obviously remembering his first influences, Benny Carter and Charlie Parker. At the end of his life, he composed the music for *Big Man*, a musical based upon the folk legend of John Henry, a steel-driver for the railroad, supposedly coming from Alabama.

Apart from being an outstanding jazz musician, Cannonball Adderley was an eloquent speaker. He developed the habit of explaining during concerts what his band actually was going to play and engaged in highly enjoyable commentaries in front of his audiences. He was also an important jazz ambassador and therefore frequently invited on television shows and as a guest speaker at universities. With his untimely death on August 8, 1975, caused by a sudden stroke, one of the most entertaining and educated jazz musicians in the world sadly disappeared from the stage. His body was flown back to Florida, where his remains rest at the Southside Cemetery in Tallahassee. Fortunately, he left us a great musical heritage.

***

Aberfeldy
Distillery

No.1 Spirit Still
15121 LTS

In studying the history of Aberfeldy distillery, one should take a close look at the Dewar dynasty first. Born in a poor crofter's family in 1805, John Dewar saw farming from the moment he entered this world. Coming of age, he decided that was not the job for him and became a joiner's apprentice. He worked in the town of Aberfeldy with his brother until 1828 when he changed jobs and moved to Perth where he was employed as a cellar man by his uncle Alex MacDonald, a wine merchant. It took him nine years to prove to his uncle he was worthy to become a partner, and in 1837 the company changed its name to MacDonald and Dewar.

Eventually, wanting to be on his own entirely, John founded a company in 1846, selling wine and spirits and blending whisky from 111 High Street in Perth. Being an innovator at heart, he started to sell whisky in glass bottles that carried his own name. At the time it was customary to sell straight from the cask, or even the whole cask to the lucky ones who could afford that. After a while John thought Perth not big enough for him so he hired a travelling salesman who would push Dewar's whisky throughout Scotland.

In 1871 his oldest son John Alexander joined and would inherit the small but sound liquor and wine business when his father died in 1880. Four years after that, John A.'s younger brother Tommy joined the firm and would become a legend in his own right. John A. the serious businessman now had his ideal counterpart, since Tommy was outgoing and very creative in attracting attention to their whisky. In 1885 Tommy moved to London, expecting to work with two seasoned salesmen recommended to him. Upon arrival he found out that one of them was dead and the other bankrupt.

This would challenge Tommy even more to make a success of his mission to conquer the world. It took Tommy another six years to get Dewar's introduced in the USA, with the voluntary help of legendary Scotsman Andrew Carnegie and the involuntary help of the US Press. In 1891 Carnegie ordered a small cask of Dewar's to be delivered to President Harrison, whereupon the press attacked Harrison for not supporting the indigenous bourbon. This surge of free publicity helped Tommy in quickly marketing Dewar's whisky throughout the USA, where it remains a top selling blended Scotch today.

Soon after his American success, Tommy left Scotland for a worldwide promotion tour and even found time afterwards to write about his adventures, published in 1894 under the title *A Ramble Round the Globe*.

In 1896 the Dewar brothers took a giant step forward and built their own distillery in nearby Aberfeldy, the birthplace of their father, to make single malt whisky for their now world-famous blend Dewar's White Label. The thought might have occurred to them that they didn't want to become too dependent on distilleries they couldn't control.

The company prospered until 1917 when the distillery was closed due to World War I. Two years later production restarted. In 1925 Distillers Company Ltd (currently

Diageo) bought the company. One hundred per cent of the production went for blending. In 1972 the still capacity was doubled to four stills during an extensive restoration project. That same year the floor maltings were closed and Aberfeldy started to buy malt elsewhere.

In 1991 the first official single malt distillery bottling was launched, a 15-year-old expression. The label featured a red squirrel, now an endangered species in Great Britain. They can be spotted in the woods behind the distillery. This particular single malt was part of the famed Flora & Fauna series, a name first coined by Michael Jackson.

In 1998 the company changed hands. Diageo sold Dewar's to Bacardi, together with five other malt distilleries. The Puerto Rico-based drinks giant meant well with Aberfeldy and built the beautiful visitor centre Dewar's World of Whisky in 2000. To commemorate this event, the distillery launched a 25-year-old expression of Aberfeldy.

The 15-year-old received a new packaging showing the portrait of John Dewar. This elegant single malt remains the backbone of Dewar's Blended Scotch. Today Aberfeldy comes in 12 and 21-year-old versions, with various labels, currently sporting the red squirrel again. Independent bottlings are extremely rare.

Tommy Dewar, the whisky marketing genius of the early 20th century, lives on in his many witty one-liners, called *Dewarisms* by his contemporaries. Have a quick taste:

Showcase

Do right and fear no man;
don't write and fear no woman.

Golf is not necessarily a rich man's sport;
there are plenty of poor players.

The biggest lies are told on gravestones.

Fish stimulates the brain,
but fishing stimulates the imagination.

If we are here to help others,
I often wonder what the others are here for.

***

Blue Note
Julian "Cannonball" Adderley was a great entertainer and very knowledgeable about music. Before he became a professional musician, he was a music teacher. Throughout his career, he would enlighten and delight his audience by introducing the pieces he played with an elaborate explanation. He not only showed that characteristic in front of live audiences but also appeared in television shows to educate the nation. His natural, down-home style made his music very accessible.

Similarly Tommy Dewar, founder of Aberfeldy, loved to play with the audience on a world-wide scale. Never too tired to preach the gospel of whisky. Well-liked and appreciated by many, he would be knighted in later life and remembered for his one-liners or Dewarisms.

Aberfeldy Distillery is the showcase of the Scottish industry. There is also a beautiful award winning visitor centre, Dewar's World of Whisky, where visitors even can make their own virtual blend.

Recommended listening
"Mercy, Mercy, Mercy"

Recommended dram
Aberfeldy 12-year-old

Tasting Note
Warm to gold bronze. Lively. Orange zest with a hint of smokiness. Warm. Light on the tongue, oily. Emphatically clean fruitiness. Tangerines. Trifle sponges. The finish is like biting in a kumquat. Dusty and spicy. Gently warming.

Underestimation
Hank Mobley with Jura

Although considered one of the founders of the Jazz Messengers, tenor saxophonist Hank Mobley was – unrightfully – underestimated, sometimes even neglected by the audience at large throughout his life. He was born in Eastman, Georgia on July 7, 1930, but grew up near Newark, New Jersey, in a musical family. Both his mother and grandmother, the latter a church organist, played keyboards, as well as his uncle Dave. No wonder Hank started to play piano first. He switched to tenor sax at the age of 16, having listened to sax players like Dexter Gordon and Lester Young, stimulated by his uncle. At 18 going on 19, Paul Gayten hired him to play rhythm and blues, which he continued to do between 1949 and 1951, all over the USA. According to Gayten, "Hank was beautiful, he played alto, tenor and baritone and did a lot of the writing."

In 1951 Mobley switched to jazz. Soon he played with the incredibly talented drummer Max Roach who loved his approach and tried to contract him for his quintet, but to no avail. In 1954 he found his place in the hard bop scene playing side by side with Dizzy Gillespie, Horace Silver and Art Blakey, thus being at the core of the first Jazz Messengers line up. He continued to play with Dizzy and Horace long after the first Messengers broke up.

Mobley was not only known for his melodic way of playing with a bluesy undertone but also as one of the truly fine composers of the hard bop period. He performed with many great musicians of that era, such as Freddie Hubbard, Winton Kelly and Lee Morgan. With the latter trumpet player, he would be especially productive.

In the early 1960s Mobley shortly joined Miles Davis, who was in search of a replacement for John Coltrane. Davis fired him since he could not live up to the expectations created by Coltrane. Critics often described Mobley's playing style to be in between Coltrane and Getz, which surely was not a downplay on his capabilities. He simply had a laid back non-flamboyant style, which might have been one of the reasons that it took so long before he became appreciated in a much wider circle.

His fellow musicians loved him and knew what he was capable of doing. However, since he usually played alongside the giants of jazz, he tended to be overshadowed by them. The advice his uncle Dave gave him in his early years also contributed to his attitude as a musician, "If you are with somebody who plays loud, you play soft. If somebody plays fast, you play slow. If you try to play the same thing they are playing, you're in trouble!" This philosophy of life made Hank Mobley the ideal musician's musician.

Unfortunately he would not live to see himself recognized as one of the great hard bop tenor saxophonists and composers. Problems with his lungs caused him to take an early retirement around 1975. Duke Jordan was one of the last musicians with whom he worked.

His now famous album *Another Workout* illustrates the negligence shown by the recording industry for this modest but gifted musician. Although it was recorded in 1961, it was released 24 years later, in 1985, shortly before his death.

Hank Mobley died on May 30, 1986, from pneumonia, virtually forgotten. Luckily, during the past years, there have been several signs of a Hank Mobley revival.

According to Robert Spencer in a 2004 article for *All About Jazz*, Mobley wasn't born in the right time, "Sonny Rollins owned the 1950s and John Coltrane quickly claimed the 1960s... If the great Hidden Hand had sent him [Mobley] into the world in 1910 instead of 1930, he might be recognized today as one of the all-time giants of the tenor saxophone..."

Hank Mobley was one of Michael Jackson's all-time favourites. The Grand Old Man of Whisky, always humble about his talents too, sure had a taste for the good stuff of life.

***

No. 2 Low Wines Still

Picture this. Beautiful natural surroundings, undisturbed by mass tourism, one distillery, approximately 200 inhabitants and 5,000 red deer. Welcome to the Isle of Jura, only separated by a relatively small strip of water from its larger sister Islay, but producing an entirely different type of whisky, largely underestimated. The cause might partly be the fame of its neighbours on the adjacent island, or partly the truly chequered history of the distillery. The operation even started under another name: Small Isles Distillery. When the license changed hands in 1831, the new lessee, William Abercrombie, introduced the name Isle of Jura. Until 1901 that license would change hands five times and the distillery narrowly escaped bankruptcy.

As if that were not enough, in 1901 license holder Ferguson entered an apparently unsolvable dispute with his landlord, one of the mighty Campbells, closed the distillery and shortly thereafter removed the roofs of the buildings, leaving them to be destroyed by the elements.

End of story? By no means, an entirely different story would be written in the 1940s. This time by famous novelist and social commentator George Orwell, who allegedly wrote his sombre scenario for the future in a cottage on the island, between 1946 and 1949. London was too busy for him at the time, and he confessed to wanting to be in an "unget-at-able" place. Looking at Jura's geographical position, the working title for his novel *The Last Man In Europe* seems well-chosen, but Orwell finally decided to name it *1984*.

In 1960 white knight Mackinlay & Co started to build an entirely new distillery, using the talents of the famous Scottish architect William Delmé-Evans. Three years later the first spirit would run from the two new stills.

73 years after the demolition of the first distillery, the new owners launched an 11-year-old single malt – apparently successfully, since a couple of years later, in 1978, the still capacity was doubled. However, there was to be no rest for the arisen phoenix. The ownership of the distillery continued to change hands: first through an acquisition made by Invergordon Distillers in 1985, who themselves would be bought by Whyte & Mackay (W&M) a mere eight years later. Although owning the Jura distillery since 1993, W&M was bought and sold several times, even having had an American owner for a while named Fortune Brands. Finally in 2007, after much speculation W&M was acquired by United Spirits, a company from India. At the end of 2012, behemoth Diageo teamed up with United Spirits, buying a large percentage of shares. It remains to be seen whether Diageo will keep the W&M brands.

Throughout the years various bottlings were launched, not all being noticed at large, partly because they were limited editions. The current range consists of a 10 year old, the Superstition, a 16 and a 21-year-old. One of the memorable limited bottlings is the 19-year-old "1984" from 2003, to celebrate the 100th birthday of Eric Arthur Blair, better known as the aforementioned George Orwell.

The Isle of Jura continues to honour the famous English author by running an international Writer Retreat Programme on the island, in close cooperation with Scottish Book Trust, the national agency for literature in Scotland. Meanwhile, Jura single malt is on the rise again, for which W&M's knowledgeable and entertaining master blender Richard Paterson can take considerable credit.

When on Islay, it pays to take the five-minute ferry trip from Port Askaig to Jura, followed by a 15-minute drive to Craighouse. Visit here not only to see and taste Jura's latest expressions, but also to observe Orwell's beautifully restored cottage. With only a minor edit *The Last Man in Europe* could easily be transformed into *The Last Malt in Europe*. And that is what no whisky lover ever wants to read. Luckily Orwell changed the title of his most famous novel.

***

Blue Note
Hank Mobley was one of the founding fathers of the hard bop with the Jazz Messenger's first line-up, consisting of famous names such as pianist Horace Silver and drummer Art Blakey. He continued to play alongside many other famous jazzmen and was highly regarded by his colleagues but hardly noticed by the audience. His playing was always

precise; he hit the right note at the right time, but in a laid-back, almost subdued manner. When he died in 1986, he was largely forgotten. Fortunately, his music has been revived during the past decades, giving Mobley his rightful position in the world of jazz.

Jura suffered a similar lot. The eponymous island is neighbour to the Isle of Islay that harbours some of the most famous, by some called notorious, of single malts: the heavily peated ones. Standing in their shadow, Jura had to create its own market. Under a new owner a brand new distillery was built in 1960, and gradually Jura regained a following of its own. It is a tender malt that needs time to be fully recognized.

Recommended listening
"I Should Care"

Recommended dram
Jura Superstition

Tasting Note
Bronze satin. Very light peat smoke, but also some sherryish sweetness. Sweet hay. Smoot and waxy body. Piney, honeyish. Developing sweet creaminess. Opens very slowly. The finish is salty, with a surprising sting.

Variations on a Theme
Art Tatum with Bowmore

The eighth wonder of the world, as Count Basie called Art Tatum, Jr., was born on October 13, 1909, in Toledo, Ohio. Being blessed with an incredible sense of hearing, already at the age of three (!), Tatum could play by ear the piano roll recordings from his mother's collection. His perfect pitch probably compensated for the fact that he was virtually blind. Turning six years old he developed such an incredible speed and accuracy that he played compositions originally meant as duets, not even aware of the fact they were meant for two piano players.

His great inspiration was Fats Waller, the best stride pianist around at the time. When Tatum joined a cutting contest in 1933, he played against his hero and was propelled into stardom almost immediately. Throughout the years, he has influenced many jazz musicians, not only pianists. Alto saxophonist Charlie Parker is reputed to have said once, "I wish I could play like Tatum's right hand." What made Art Tatum so unique was not only his incredible speed and accuracy, but also his capability to create a distinctive swing element in his piano sound. When playing jazz solos, he never forgot the original melody of the song on which he was improvising, and he is credited for innovative harmonization by changing the chord progressions sustaining the melodies.

Recordings of his work are mostly solo piano. There was hardly a musician who could keep up with his tempo of playing. However, he did form a trio in the early 1940s with Tiny Grimes on guitar and Slam Stewart on bass. On some of those recordings, the latter two can literally be heard to more or less run behind Tatum. The blind pianist with the perfect pitch was so accurate that the majority of his solo recordings were done in one take.

Many of his compositions were transcribed, but few would actually try and practice his pieces, since they were extremely difficult to play. Many critics agree that Tatum would provide the bebop generation the material with which they could exercise, thus becoming the great inspiration of bebop way before the actual style came into fruition. Charlie Parker, who else, would be one of his greatest advocates about 20 years later.

Among the pianists who would interpret and play his pieces was Oscar Peterson. When he heard Tatum for the first time, Peterson became so frightened that he didn't touch the piano for a couple of months. Luckily Oscar made up for it until his death in December 2007.

In the Broadway and classical realm Tatum was admired too. Rubinstein and Gershwin, for instance, and Vladimir Horowitz, of whom it was said that he was moved to tears upon hearing Tatum for the first time and remarked that the classically trained pianists were lucky that he hadn't pursued a career in classical music.

The biggest compliment, however, came from Tatum's all-time hero, Fats Waller. When playing in a club in 1938, Waller noticed that Art Tatum had entered and told the audience at once, "I just play the piano, but God is in the house tonight."

Tatum didn't grow old. Having been a heavy drinker most of his working life he suffered from kidney problems and died in Los Angeles of uraemia on November 5, 1956, only 47 years old.

His name not only lives on in his music but in a musical term too. A student of the Massachusetts Institute of Technology introduced it in 1993 when he defined the Tatum as "the smallest perceptual time unit in music." A truly remarkable way to be remembered.

Art Tatum's final resting place is at the Forest Lawn Memorial Park Cemetery in Glendale, California.

***

The village of Bowmore at Loch Indaal is considered the "capital" of the Isle of Islay and was founded in 1768, although there was already a pier in 1750. The man who constructed the village was Daniel Campbell of Shawfield. He was a man with a vision and a mission. This branch of the Campbells has done a lot to improve the living conditions on Islay. An obelisk at Bridgend reminds the islanders of what this family did throughout the ages.

Bowmore is designed on a rectangular grid, and its main street leads up to the famous round church, built without corners to prevent the devil from hiding. A local legend tells that Satan tried to hide but to no avail. Instead, parishioners chased the devil into the streets from which he ran inside the distillery, never to be found. It is whispered that he made his escape in a cask that was shipped to the mainland shortly thereafter.

Jumping from lore to truth, it may be said with certainty that Bowmore Distillery is the oldest one on Islay. Founded 11 years after the building of the village had started, it was run by its founder until 1837, in which year the distillery was sold to Mr William Mutter of Glasgow. Mutter kept the distillery for 55 years and did extensive construction work, expanding the capacity. In 1892 a group of English businessmen took over and held the distillery for the next 33 years. J. B. Sheriff and Company would buy Bowmore in 1925, to hold it only for four years, when the Distillers Company Ltd (DCL, a forerunner of Diageo) acquired the distillery in 1929.

This wasn't the end of changing hands for Bowmore. In 1950 William Grigor & Son took over, managing the distillery for thirteen years. In 1963 Stanley P. Morrison paid the then princely sum of £ 117,000 for lock, stock and barrel. He ran Bowmore for more than a quarter century. In 1989 he decided to literally bring in foreign capital and invited the Japanese drinks giant Suntory to become a 35% shareholder.

Apparently the Japanese liked what they saw, since they acquired the remaining 65% in 1994. They must love the place, since they spent millions to improve the site, reopening an entirely refurbished visitor centre in 2006. One of few in the trade, Bowmore's malting floor is still intact and provides 38% of the malted barley needed by the distillery. The rest is supplemented by Port Ellen Maltings. The whisky is well liked by aficionados as well as collectors. Belgian Whisky buff Bob Minnekeer earns his nickname Bowmore Bob and has an impressive range of bottlings on display in his Glengarry whisky club in Ghent, Belgium. The late Dutch collector and liquor specialist Harry Verhaar left a beautiful collection of Bowmore paraphernalia to his son Marcel, who still takes care of his father's legacy. Another collector, Dutchman Hans Sommer, sold his entire collection to the distillery in 2004. It consists of more than 200 different expressions, one of them being the famous Black Bowmore bottling from 1993, also released in 1994 and 1995. At the end of 2007 this cult edition was re-released in a very limited amount, a 43 year old from 1964.

Bowmore has always had an impressive range of expressions but decided in 2006 to concentrate on fewer versions. The current output, however, is still considerable and consists of two different series, one for the normal retail and one for travel retail outlets. The line up of the core range now is Legend, 12, 18 and 25 year old, a 16-year-old Port-matured, and the 15-year-old Darkest. In travel retail the following expressions can be spotted: Surf, Enigma, Mariner 15 year old, the famed 17 year old and a cask strength version. Also several independent bottlings may be obtained, most notably from Duncan Taylor, Douglas Laing and Cadenhead.

It looks as if one may swim in the many varieties, which is no exaggeration, especially as one really can take a dive at Bowmore. One of the warehouses was converted into a swimming pool for the inhabitants of the village in 1991. The pool is heated with recycled hot water from the distillery. It gives a new meaning to the expression "water of life."

***

Blue Note
Art Tatum, an enthusiastic imbiber of the cratur, was an amazing, almost blind pianist, who would take on any challenge in a piano stride. He primarily recorded solo piano pieces, but also recorded with a trio. Usually the

bass player and drummer couldn't keep up with him. Art Tatum is credited with heavily influencing his successors who all gave him praise for his enormous capability of creating new harmonies without losing track of the original theme.

Darkest, Dusk, Dawn, Legend, Surf, Black Bowmore. The list of various bottlings is too long to mention here. The many expressions from the oldest distillery on Islay vary in taste, but carry the distinctive flavour that makes them all recognizable members of the same family: Bowmore Distillers. A harmonic dram, well balanced. The output of new variations is up to speed, probably only surpassed in tempo by Bruichladdich on the other side of Loch Indaal.

Recommended listening
"Tiger Rag"

Recommended dram
Bowmore 17-year-old

Tasting Note
Full gold to bronze. Smoothly aromatic. Nutty malt. Smoky. Medicinal Islay character. Light to medium body, but smooth and firm. Malty, dry creaminess. Tightly combined flavours. The finish is leafy, ferny, malty, sandy and smoky. Slightly astringent.

Acknowledgements

During research and writing this book I was helped by many people. I would like to thank the following for their contributions:

Ronald Anneveldt, Celine Antoine, Carol Bennet, Isabelle Berendsen, Dave Broom, Ian Buxton, Ronnie Cox, Peter Currie, Mitchell Davis, Liddy Dragt, Theo Dragt†, Jane Grimley, Marcel van Gils, Harry de Graaf, staff and regulars at pub De Tagrijn, Peter Guthrie, Kevin Hamilton, James Hershorn, Jos Huigsloot, Michael Jackson†, Eric Jefferson, Romain Larcheron, Gert van der Linden, Anja van Loon, Graham Logie, Eddie MacAffer, John MacDonald, Jamie MacKenzie, John MacLellan, Ian McArthur, Jack McCray†, Deneen McElveen, Barbara & Jim McEwan, Duncan McGillavry, Frank McHardy, Elaine Morrirson, Herman Nijkamp, Becky Lovett Offringa, Sue Pettit, Erik Raayman, Mark Reynier, Leen Ripke, Jacco van Santen, Pieter van Santen, Charlton Singleton, Carol Smagalsky, Lee Tanner, Gary Taylor, Serge Valentin, Charles Waring III, Ben Williams, Ronald Zwartepoorte.

Bibliography

<u>Books</u>

Barnard, Alfred. *The Whisky Distilleries of the United Kingdom*, originally published in 1887. Facsimile reprint from 2000 by Gunnar Kwisinski & Jens Sagemann. ISBN 3934005845.

Broom, Dave. *The World Atlas of Whisky*. Mitchell Beazley, 2010. ISBN 978 1 84533 5410.

Gilbert, Will G. E and Mr. C. Poustochkine. *Jazzmuziek.* J. Philip Kruseman's Publishers. N.V. 1948. No ISBN.

Harris, Rex. *Jazz*, 4th edition. Penguin Books Ltd. 1956. No ISBN, referenced as a Pelican Book, number A247.

Jackson, Michael. *The Malt Whisky Companion*, 5th edition. Dorling Kindersley, 2004. ISBN 1405302348.

Jackson, Michael. *WHISKY The Definitive World Guide.* Dorling Kindersley, 2005. ISBN 0751344346.

Kircher, Bill. *The Oxford Companion to Jazz.* Oxford University Press, 2000. ISBN 9780195183597.

Ronde, Ingvar. *Malt Whisky Yearbook.* MagdigMedia Ltd, 2013. ISBN 9780955 260797.
Shipton, Alyn. *A New History of Jazz.* Continuum, in association with Bayou Press Ltd, 2001. ISBN 0826447546.

Udo, Misako. *The Scottish Whisky Distilleries.* Distillery Cat Publishing, 2005. ISBN 0955062209.

Ward, Geoffrey C. and Ken Burns. *JAZZ: A History of America's Music.* Alfred E. Knopf Publishers, 2000. ISBN 067944551X.

DVDs
Burns, Ken. *JAZZ: A History of America's Music.*
A set of 10 DVDs, accompaniment to the eponymous book.

Websites

http://afgen.com/milt.html

http://az.essortment.com/stangetzbiogr_rybw.htm

www.allaboutjazz.com

www.artieshaw.com

www.balblair.com

www.bowmore.co.uk

www.bruichladdich.com

www.bunnahabhain.com

www.cannonball-adderley.com

www.chetbakertribute.com

www.cmgww.com/music/parker/

www.dewars.com

www.dextergordon.com

www.duke.edu/~njh3/biography.html

www.glenrothes.com

www.islayinfo.com

www.isleofjura.com

www.jazzdisco.org

www.jazz.org

www.johncoltrane.com

www.malts.com

www.milesdavis.com

www.springbankdistillers.com

www.wikipedia.org

www.wright.edu/~martin.maner/mobley.htm

Photo Registry

Other Works by the Author

English Books

A Taste of Whisky	2007
The Book of CEOs	2000
Bourbon & Blues	2011
Cowbook	2001
Raising The Kursk *(+ DVD)*	2003
Craigellachie Collection of Scotch Whisky Labels	1998
The House – A Moving Story	2000
The Legend of Laphroaig	2007
The Malt Log	2012
The Road to Craigellachie	2005
The Road to Craigellachie – Revisited	2011
Rum & Reggae	2013
Whisky & Jazz	2009

Dutch Books

De Berging van de Koersk *(+ DVD)*	2003
Bourbon & Blues *(Deel 2 Drank & Klank Trilogie)*	2011
Champagne de Luxe – De Smaak, De Traditie	2010
Classic Malts Selection	2005
The Famous Scheurkalender I	2011
The Famous Scheurkalender II	2012
Golf The Box – Hoe & Waarom?	2011
Golf The Box – Wie, Wat, Waar?	2011
Het Groot Directeuren Boek	1998, 2007

Het Gecomponeerde Kleinkind	2005
Het Huis	1997, 2010
Ik kom uit Zwolle, vette pech	2004
Koeboek	1999, 2007
Malts & Jazz *(Deel 1 Drank & Klank Trilogie)*	2012
Men neme Malt	2008
Nightcaps	2007
Rum & Reggae *(Deel 3 Drank & Klank Trilogie)*	2012
Schotse Whisky – The Box: Blended Whisky	2009
Schotse Whisky – The Box: Malt Whisky	
Schotse Whisky – The Box: Proeven van Schotland	
Sint Bonifatiuspark	2008
De Smaak van Whisky	2007
Stokpaardjes	2007
Het Vertrek	2003, 2010
De Weg naar Craigellachie	2004
Whisky Almanak 1e editie & 2de editie	2005 & 2006
Whisky Scheurkalender I & II	2005 & 2007
Whisky & Jazz	2009
De Zes Pijlers van The Macallan	2011
Zwolle, een smakelijk stukje historie	2003

French Books

Classic Malts Selection	2005
Malts & Merveilles	2008

Co-author

Beer Hunter, Whisky Chaser (I. Buxton et al)	2009
Whisky – Eyewitness Guide (C. Maclean et al)	2008

Other Works by the Author

WORLD WHISKY (C Maclean et al)	2009
1001 Whiskies to Try Before You Die (D. Roskrow et al)	2012
Whisky The World Atlas (D. Broom) (*photos*)	2010

Translated Books

De Malt Whisky Companion (Michael Jackson)	2006
Focus Whisky (Charles Maclean et al)	2008
Whisky de Wereldatlas (Dave Broom)	2011
Whisky Encyclopedie (Michael Jackson)	2005
Single Malt Whisky (David Wishart)	2003
Whisky Geclassificeerd 1e editie (D. Wishart)	2003
Whisky Geclassificeerd 2e editie (D. Wishart)	2006
Whisky Mini Winkler Prins (Carol Shaw)	2003

Articles for newspapers, magazines and websites
Angels Share
Charleston Mercury
InCt
Kiln
Levenswater
WFNN
Whisky Advocate
Whisky Etc.
Whiskyforum
Whisky Magazine
Whisky Pages
Whisky Passion

www.hansoffringa.com.